9-CCA-374

A BLANDFORD
GARDENING HANDBOOK

WATER GARDENING

Peter McHoy

BLANDFORD PRESS
POOLE · NEW YORK · SYDNEY

First published in the UK 1986 by Blandford Press,
Link House, West Street, Poole, Dorset, BH15 1LL

Distributed in the United States by
Sterling Publishing Co., Inc.,
2 Park Avenue, New York, N.Y. 10016

Distributed in Australia by
Capricorn Link (Australia) Pty Ltd
PO Box 665, Lane Cove, NSW 2066

British Library Cataloguing in Publication Data

McHoy, Peter
  Water gardening.—(A Blandford gardening handbook)
  1. Water gardens
  I. Title
  635.9′674   SB423

ISBN 0 7137 1577 4 (Hardback)
    0 7137 1484 4 (Paperback)

All photographs by Peter McHoy. Colour and
line artwork by Paula Chasty. The author
would like to thank the following for sharing their experience
of water plants: Mr R. Davies (Stapeley Water Gardens),
Mr J. Bennett (Bennett's Water Lily Farm), and Mr Grubb
(Newlake Gardens).

Typeset by Megaron Typesetting, Bournemouth, Dorset

Printed in Portugal by Printer Portuguesa

CONTENTS

INTRODUCTION

Read any book about water gardening, and you will find the same recurring theme: that water has a special fascination for almost all of us. This book is no exception, and elsewhere the same claims are made. The reason is simple: it is true.

I have certainly spent more hours gazing within the depth of my pools, or simply 'pottering about with ponds', than I have spent enjoying any other garden feature, and any water project has always met with enthusiasm from the

In an established pond, most of the water area is covered by plants.

whole family. Quite simply water gardening is exciting.

The discovery of the first of the season's frog spawn, the excitement of the realisation that suddenly there are literally hundreds of baby fish, are aspects of water gardening that typify the ever-changing and very dynamic nature of this form of gardening.

Even if you dispense with fish and wildlife, the *sound* of water from say a cascade or fountain will again bring life and movement to the garden.

As an element in garden design, water can play an essential role. It did in the great landscape gardens of past generations, and it still does today in the infinitely smaller modern garden. If you doubt this, look at the illustrations in any garden design book or think about the display gardens at some of the biggest flower shows. Few garden designers can resist the temptation to include water somewhere.

Enthusiasm alone will not build your water garden, of course. Nor will it guarantee success (and let no-one doubt that there can be failures and disappoint-

A cascade on this scale will need a very powerful pump and it is best to consult a water garden specialist at an early stage.

ments). It has been the aim throughout this book to keep one's feet firmly on the ground. If something is expensive, I have said so. If a job is really hard work, I have said so (and usually been able to suggest an alternative). If you are likely to run into problems, I have said so.

In our list of plants, which includes all those that you are likely to find in the water garden department of a garden centre or at a water-garden specialist, you will find less space devoted to written descriptions of the plants than in many books, but a real appraisal of what you can really expect from the plants. Some that look superb as illustrations in books may take many years to reach that stage; you will find a guide to how quickly you can expect results. To help you find the real winners from the 'also-rans', a rating

has been given based on the combined practical experience of several of the largest aquatic plant growers.

If this is your first pond, there should be all the guidance you need. There should also be plenty to interest even the converted.

POND OR POOL?

The terms pond and pool are used interchangeably in most books on water gardens, but unaware of this readers sometimes assume some difference is intended (perhaps that one is natural, the other man-made). Lest anyone be in doubt, there is no difference, and the use of both 'pool' and 'pond' is to avoid constant repetition of the same word.

1·THE ATTRACTIONS OF WATER GARDENING

Water has many attractions. Even non-gardeners will be quick to extoll its fascination, and children who may not develop a real interest in gardening for another twenty years will usually be pleased to spend more than a few hours helping with a pond or a stream.

To suggest that ponds are for the young at heart or playthings for the non-gardeners among us would be to miss the major contribution that water features make to good garden design and to denigrate an absorbing and serious hobby in its own right. The truth is that water gardening has a broad-based appeal, and it has different attractions for different people. To that extent it can be much more of a family activity than say rock or greenhouse gardening. There are families who have devoted almost the whole garden to ponds, where one person is in charge of the fish-keeping and the 'mechanics' of pump and water maintenance, and another is in charge of the aquatic plants. Even where the pond forms a more modest proportion of the garden, and the owners are less dedicated, a water feature can be fun for the whole family (and not least the children, who one can almost guarantee will take an intense interest in it from the moment the idea of a pond is mooted).

Water gardening books generally concentrate on either the plants (and it will stagger most gardeners to know that some of them list well over 150 varieties of waterlilies) or on the pond as a habitat for wildlife. The aim of this book is to set the water garden in the wider context of the garden as a whole, and as a potential source of fascination for anyone who cares to look beneath the surface.

Later chapters deal in detail with the specific aspects of water gardening: from

Water features can be effective with neither fish nor plants. The sound of the three small fountains adds much to the atmosphere in this formal pool.

construction and stocking to wildlife and cleaning and renovating. This chapter is intended to answer some of the doubts a prospective first-time pond-owner might have, and reveal some additional and perhaps unexpected benefits.

WATER IN DESIGN

You can come to the conclusion that you need a pond purely on the grounds that the idea appeals. Some are introduced to the delights of water gardening not by

Water does not have to be deep to be interesting. In this design for a roof garden, where weight is a major consideration, the water is only a couple of inches deep, but the black liner gives the impression of greater depth.

Raised pools can be particularly interesting because they bring the water closer to eye level.

any instinctive love of water or wildlife but by basic design needs; in other words the water is a functional part of the garden design. You can have the best of both worlds: water because you like it, while at the same time improving the garden as a whole.

There is no single right approach; to the real enthusiast with a desire to have as much aquatic potential as possible, overall garden design may be unimportant, and certainly sterile formal pools and bubble fountains would hardly be rated very highly. For the garden designer, however, shape, sound and style will be uppermost.

It is never a good idea to ignore good design principles, and a designer should never ignore the importance of water.

Water is a very dominant design feature. It often has a significance far beyond its size. Apart from the visual attraction of the pool in its own right, water has the useful attribute of reflecting light, and running water inevitably draws attention. Like all good things, it can be overdone of course, and in a small garden it is best to use water in a formal way, even if in rectangular or circular, possibly interlinking, pools.

Rock gardens and ponds associate well together, and weatherworn limestone links the two particularly well.

It is worth taking some trouble to integrate the pond with the rest of the garden, and careful planting at the pond-edge and around the pond can play an important role.

Alternatively 'water sculpture' (see illustration on page 9) or a simple bubble fountain may be sufficient from a garden design viewpoint if not from the water gardener's standpoint. Avoid the temptation to scoff at something modest as lacking interest; although you might find the possibilities of say a cut-down barrel pool, or even a plastic container, rather restricting, they can be a lot of fun. They can look attractive too (see pages 21 and 29).

Formal pools should conform to a geometric shape, and have a crisp outline. They can be particularly effective raised rather than sunken; and of course there is the advantage of bringing many of the pleasures of the pond nearer to eye level. As walls of raised pools have to be reasonably wide they also provide a convenient place to pause and sit for a while.

Informal pools generally need a garden of more generous proportions unless worked into the design very skilfully. To sustain a natural effect the planting should also be informal.

STILL OR MOVING WATER

There are practical considerations discussed in later chapters that might affect your decision (waterlilies prefer still water for instance), but it is worth looking first at the design considerations that might also influence your judgement.

Beware of fountains. They can look contrived in an informal pool and either pathetic if underpowered or pretentious if too powerful. The most successful types of fountains in a small garden are either geysers or water spouts (the latter perhaps playing diagonally across a formal pool). It is the scaled-down versions of the more classic fountain displays that are at the same time the most tempting to buy and the least likely to be successful in garden design terms.

A cascade of some kind can usually be incorporated satisfactorily, whatever the size and style of garden, and this may be a more successful way of providing the sight and sound of moving water. In a

A bubble fountain – a water feature that you may consider safe even if you have small children. It gives you the sight and sound of running water with few dangers.

Goldfish basking in the summer sunshine.

large garden, an informal water garden with 'stream' and waterfall may be feasible, but even in a small garden a series of small formal pools can be very successful with water cascading from one to another over lips.

Although garden design is beyond the scope of this book, it will be clear that a sympathetic approach is needed if water is to enhance the garden and not to detract from the other features.

ANIMAL LIFE

The idyllic image of colourful fish merrily splashing about at the surface as a contribution to the garden scene is best forgotten. It happens, and when it does it really is a joy, but for most of the time for most of the days, and certainly during the winter, the pond can seem devoid of animal inhabitants from a distance. This is why it should be looked at within the context of the overall garden design.

Unless you sterilise the pool to keep the water in a formal feature clear and pure, however, the pond will be teeming with both animal and plant life, even without conscious help on your part. Once stocked with fish and aquatic plants there will never be a dull moment for anyone with eyes to see.

You will undoubtedly come to know the mating calls of frogs, and on the right night go out to find more frogs than you thought existed in the neighbourhood. There will be the inevitable frog spawn and tadpoles, but more exciting the thrill of suddenly being aware of baby fish, so tiny that they look like a pair of big eyes on a thread.

Birds will be attracted to the garden too; not only birds that one associates

13

This small raised pond has well-established plants that give it a surprisingly natural appearance.

A tropical waterlily, 'Director Moore'. Although you need a warm greenhouse for tropical waterlilies, they can be grown in bowls and put outdoors for the warmest few months.

with water (with luck not the heron), but all kinds of other birds that will come to drink, especially during the summer.

Dragonflies will appear (be prepared for a shock if you have never seen the very ugly nymphs that will be the result of their visits), and for the inquisitive there will be numerous water insects to be identified. Somehow these always seem more interesting than the even greater number of insects that you will undoubtedly find in the rest of the garden.

The fish can even become pets; if you have the patience some of them can be tamed to feed from your fingers.

PLANTS

Although newts and water-boatmen might be a source of endless enjoyment for the young-at-heart or the inquisitive, to many gardeners they will be mere incidentals if not a nuisance. For a true gardener, water gardening offers an opportunity to grow an even wider range of plants, among them some of the most beautiful in the plant kingdom, of which the waterlily must take pride of place. *So what are the drawbacks?* This book has set out to be realistic in its approach. Dreams are more likely to come true if you know what is achievable in real life and what you can discount as wishful thinking.

There are problems, or rather frustrations. In later chapters there are suggestions for solving most of them, but some are either intractable or limitations that you have to accept.

Green or cloudy water is something that nobody wants but everybody gets at some time. It is no use hoping it will not happen to *your* pond: it will, and you must know how to get the better of it. Usually the problem is easily solved,

A tropical pond. This is a large one, but you can grow most of these plants just as well in a pool in a conservatory or greenhouse.

given a little time, but sometimes it can be a stubborn problem.

Another problem is the slow rate of growth of some of the plants. There are rapid-growers of course (which you may later regret planting), but many of the choice plants that you see as magnificent clumps in illustrations may take years to reach that stage. Sadly there is no substitute for patience, but the sooner you get started, the sooner you will have a mature water garden.

A TROPICAL POND

There is another branch of water gardening that you may not have thought about but which is worth considering if you have a heated greenhouse or conservatory. A 'tropical' pond will give you an opportunity to grow blue waterlilies, to flower water hyacinths easily (they can be infuriatingly difficult to flower outdoors), and to enjoy active fish over a much longer period. Although a proper pool in a conservatory is ideal, you can grow your tropical waterlilies in washing-up bowls in the greenhouse.

2·PLANNING A POND

Assuming you have convinced yourself of the desirability of a pond, or other water feature, there comes the question of size, materials, cost, and probably site if this has not already been selected. Site needs careful consideration, for it is not only a matter of suiting the overall garden design (see Chapter 1), but also what suits the plants and fish.

The more open the site, and the more sun it receives, the better. Waterlilies in particular enjoy plenty of sun, and livestock generally will thrive more readily. Few bog plants, and hardly any aquatics, will flower well in shade. If compromise is necessary, try to ensure that the pond

Sometimes a simple bubble type fountain is much more effective and in keeping with the setting than a traditional spray fountain.

will receive at least five hours of direct sunlight during the summer. Only as a last resort have a pond close to trees. Not only will they cast shade, and the roots possibly interfere with some types of pond construction materials, but the leaves will be a source of constant irritation in the autumn as they have to be controlled if the water is not to become polluted.

It may be better to think again if the only site seems to be close to trees: rather than risk the disappointment that is likely to follow, see whether there is a more suitable form of water gardening, such as a pool in a barrel, maybe an indoor pool in a conservatory, or even a simple bubble fountain if you are prepared to sacrifice the fish and the plants.

Siting an informal pool needs particular care. A formal pond can usually be accommodated quite happily, provided it fits in with the overall design of the garden, without offending visually. An informal pool will look contrived and wrong unless it follows the laws of nature. It ought to be towards the lowest part of the garden if possible, not at the top of a slope. This will also help, of course, if you want to introduce cascades.

Accessibility is important too. There is not a lot of point in having a pond that you seldom see. Ideally you should be able to view it from the house, although this may be an advantage that you have to sacrifice for a sunny position.

A pond will act like a magnet in summer, and if you are not careful there will be a track made across the grass unless there is adequate footpath access.

Perhaps the most compelling reasons for having a pond somewhere near the house if possible are the practical ones of providing a power supply for pumps and lights, and for filling and topping up the pool it needs to be within reach of a reasonable length of hose-pipe.

SIZE

For anyone making their first pond there will be a temptation to make it small. It

Few of us can plan our garden with the water as well integrated with the overall design and planting as this example, but it always pays to look at a water feature within the overall garden design.

17

An informal pond. If you have a large pond you can grow some of the large, vigorous waterlilies.

on the ground – as a rectangle 3×1.5 m (10×5 ft) or a circle with a diameter of 2.4 m (8 ft) – and it will not seem particularly generous.

SHAPE

The shape of a formal pool will be dictated to a large extent by the overall design of the garden. Rectangles are usually used, but octagonal and round pools are just a couple of the other shapes that might be used. An L-shaped pond can be particularly effective, and a half-circle raised pond perhaps with a small water spout from a mask combines a sort of formality with a relaxed style.

Informal ponds need more careful thought. Certainly any curves should be gradual and laid to a radius, or a series of radii. Resist the temptation to go for too many scallops and narrow 'waists'. They may look interesting on paper, or in a pre-formed pool standing on end at a garden centre. It will seem different when the pond is viewed at a normal angle in the ground.

Some of these shortcomings will be obvious if the shape is pegged out on the ground and then marked out with a clothes-line or something similar. Remember, too, when you look at it from a low angle, that the level of water will probably be a couple of inches below the edge and that will accentuate the problem in the narrow parts as the water may hardly be visible from a distance.

Keep the shape as uncomplicated and

will seem less of a commitment if things do not work out as expected, and of course it will be cheaper. Preformed pools out of the ground at a garden centre or display ground also look deceptively big; only when they are in the ground do they seem suddenly much smaller than you had imagined.

Unfortunately a small pond will have many more problems than a large one, and that may be enough to deter one from taking the next step. A small pond will be very difficult to 'balance', the pool will probably remain green and murky most of the time, and the range of fish and plants that can be accommodated will be depressingly small.

Any minimum size must be a subjective judgement, and rather arbitrary, but 4.5 m² (50 sq ft) of surface area is about the minimum that it is sensible to aim for. This may sound large, but peg it out

Water as a formal feature, very much part of an integrated design.

simple as possible: the wider the expanse of water the more effective it will look. The shapes that will give you the maximum expanse of water looked at from any angle are circles and squares.

You will want to avoid these in an informal pool, but the principle is worth remembering, along with the importance of gradual curves laid to a definite radius. By the time plants have grown along the edge it will look irregular and informal enough.

Forget any ideas of bridges or islands

Formal pond shapes

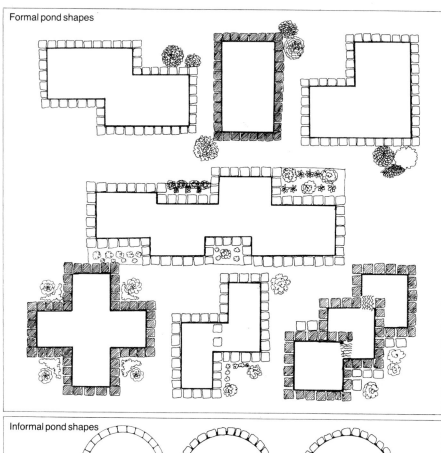

Informal pond shapes

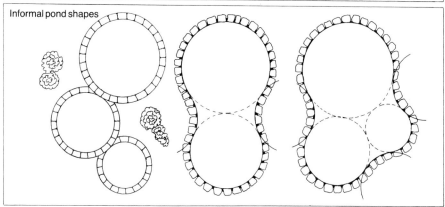

A selection of ideas for formal and informal pool shapes. There are obviously almost endless permutations, and these are just a few ideas that you may be able to adapt to suit your own garden. Bear in mind that ponds with a curved outline will generally be much more successful if the curves are made to a radius (two of the illustrations of informal pools demonstrate how this can work).

unless you have a large garden and a pond to match.

DEPTH

Visually depth is not important. If you use a black liner, a pond only 7.5 – 10 cm (3 – 4 in) deep can be very effective visually. It will not be much good for

supporting fish or plants, but as a setting for playing water, or to act as a reflective pool in a formal design setting, it may be all that is necessary.

No garden pool really needs to be deeper than 75 cm (2½ ft). The vast majority of waterlilies need a pond depth of less than 45 cm (1½ ft), and even the vigorous kinds will grow happily in a pond 60 cm (2 ft) deep. That also allows for the depth of the planting basket.

It is sometimes thought that fish need deep water, mainly as protection during cold weather. In a temperate climate ice is very unlikely to form more than say 23 cm (9 in) thick. More important than the thickness of the ice is the build-up of toxic gases and the lack of oxygen

Excavating a pond is hard work, and a pickaxe will be invaluable for breaking up hard ground.

A half-barrel pond. A surprising number of plants can be grown in a container like this.

A simple but very effective pool, ideal for this sort of natural setting.

beneath the ice; a problem that will be there whether there is 30 cm or 60 cm of water beneath the ice. The important thing is to keep some of the ice open (see pages 117-19) if the surface is frozen over for a prolonged period (it will not matter for a day or two).

Bear in mind, also, that the deeper the water the more difficult it will be to see and appreciate many of the fish (even with 'clear' water).

Taking the lawn right up to the water's edge looks good, but you will have to use a grass-box if the clippings are not to fall into the water.

A formal pool where the water acts very much as a centrepiece for the surrounding garden.

There *are* problems with making the pond too shallow, of course. Some fish do prefer a good depth of water (large Koi carp for instance), and depth will affect the control of algae and the temperature of the water. The shallower the pool the less volume of water there is to absorb the sun's light penetration and heating effect, so algae may thrive and multiply more rapidly. The temperature of the water is likely to fluctuate more rapidly than in a deeper pool. None of this will matter where the water is to be kept sterile with chemicals, but it affects the pond balance where livestock and plants are concerned.

As a guide, aim for 45 cm (1½ ft) if you want to be fairly confident of a trouble-free pond; 60 cm (2 ft) is better; anything deeper might help the overall balance of the pool, assuming a proportional surface area, but involves increased construction

23

work and expense with rapidly decreasing benefits.

There are exceptions to these guidelines. It is possible to have a 'stream' as shallow as say 25 cm (10 in) without undue problems, provided that it is linked to a pond of adequate depth and water is circulated between them with a pump (at least in the summer). The possibilities for fish are of course limited in this depth, but you can achieve a good display of marginal plants.

It is easy to overlook the effect of sloping sides on pool capacity. A saucer-shaped pool will not only reduce the volume of water but also increase the algae problem, because the shallow areas will allow light and warmth from the sun to penetrate the depth more easily.

Sides should be as steep as the construction method will allow – usually an angle of about 20 degrees (1 in 3 in) is ideal.

calculate, but the more intricate the shape the more guesswork is involved.

The volume (how many gallons or litres it holds) is important for all kinds of reasons (not least of which is calculating the dose if you have to treat the pond with chemicals).

Having worked out the surface area in feet, multiply this by the average depth. Multiply this answer by 6.25 for Imperial gallons, by 7.5 for US gallons or 28.4 for litres. It is worth making a note of the volume and keeping it in a safe place to save recalculating it next time you need to know.

If you know the volume and the surface area you can easily calculate how many gallons the pond holds for each sq ft of surface. Less than 7 gallons/sq ft is likely to lead to problems. Anything over 10 gallons/sq ft should be trouble-free. Anything between these two figures should be adequate.

VOLUME-SURFACE RATIO

This is not a very precise measure for most ponds, because of sloping sides and sometimes intricate shapes, but nevertheless some idea of the volume-surface ratio is very useful in deciding whether the pond is likely to be problem-free or troublesome.

The surface area is of course simple to calculate: just multiply length by width. Straightforward if the pond is a rectangle, not so easy if it is an irregular shape. It is still usually relatively easy to

EFFORT AND ENERGY

The days when pond-making meant concrete mixing have gone, but let no-one think that making a pond (even with modern materials) is without effort. Excavating the hole calls for muscle-power, and on some soils it can be a long and tedious job, calling for pick-axe as well as spade.

Installing a pond can be a job completed in hours . . . once the hole is dug. For a large pond it may be best to spread the excavation work over several months if your muscles are not accustomed to this sort of work. If you are simply not up to this kind of physical effort, consider having someone do it for you; a garden contractor will take the soil away for you too if you do not have any other use for it.

You can, of course, reduce the amount of excavation by building a raised pond, but you will still have bricks or blocks to manhandle and concrete and mortar to mix. It will almost certainly be a lengthier job than a sunken pond, so this is no easy option.

If it all seems rather hard work, there is the consolation that, once constructed, a pond will need very little maintenance, and should be a lot less effort to look after than say a lawn or flower beds and borders.

Plenty of plant growth is important for healthy pond life. Although this is primarily a fish-keeper's pond, it still has plenty of water plants.

A bubble fountain helps to create interest and oxygenates the water in a heavily stocked pool.

COST

Water gardening can seem expensive. That is because the heavy expenditure all comes at the beginning.

The cost of the pond itself, or a liner, has to be faced. You can make a cheap pond using polythene as a liner, but any serious pond owner is going to want something longer-lasting, and that means more expensive materials. It is possible to spend as much again on a pump for a cascade or fountain, and if you are both

A mountain stream recreated. This sort of feature needs plenty of skill to construct and a powerful pump.

impatient and rich you can spend more than £1,000 on a single Koi carp (on the other hand you can buy a young one for less than the price of a common goldfish).

You can spread some of the costs of course; the pump can wait a year (you will have lots to interest you in the meantime), and accessories such as underwater lighting (if you really want it) could wait for yet another season.

Once you have bought your liner or pre-formed shell, the annual expenditure on a water garden will not be much. It will give lots of pleasure and be undemanding on both purse and time.

27

3·MAKING A POND

Dreaming about a pond, visualising the various options in your own garden, is always fun. There comes a point, however, at which realities have to be faced: what it will cost, how long it will take, what physical effort is involved, and of course the ever-pressing question of which material to use.

CHOOSING THE RIGHT MATERIAL

This has to be your first decision — on it depends the best method of construction.

You may, of course, decide that you want a preformed pool simply because it takes many of the decisions away from you and you can easily visualise the finished pond. Usually, though, cost and life expectancy weigh equally heavily. There is no one perfect solution, it all depends on what you want, what you can afford, and what effort you want to put into making your pond. Only *you* can know the answer to those questions. The summaries below should help you to come up with the right solutions.

Butyl This is placed first because the list is alphabetical, but it also happens to be the first choice of the vast majority of experienced pond owners. Certainly it

has to be high on your list of priorities if you want to use a liner. The chances are if you make a pond with one of the other liners you will be satisfied with it, but you will probably turn to butyl the next time round. It quite simply has the edge over the alternatives except in cost.

Reservoirs are sometimes made from butyl liners, so there can be no doubt of its durability. It is said to last for at least 50 years. It has not been used long enough to be precise about ultimate life expectancy, but butyl liners have been used for many years now and there is no

Pre-formed pools are not everyone's idea of aesthetic acceptability, but they are instant and you know that they will be watertight.

A plastic tub can make a pretty miniature pool.

reason to doubt that it will last most of us for a gardening lifetime. A quality butyl liner may have a 20-year guarantee, and even the lower-quality butyl liners may carry a 10-year guarantee. In comparison with other liners it is also easier to work with; it has more 'give' and will stretch into shape more easily.

Its colour, black, sounds unattractive but is really a major advantage. If the liner does show at the edge, whether through poor levelling during construction, or because the water level has dropped in hot, dry weather, black will look far less obtrusive than other colours. Black also gives an impression of greater depth, and even a shallow pool can look much deeper than its true depth.

You can buy a butyl liner with a stone-coloured backing laminated to it, but the cost is considerably higher. It still suffers the drawbacks of all pale liners, and hardly seems worth such a premium in cost.

Nothing is perfect of course, and if you go prodding about in the bottom of the pond with a garden fork the liner is likely to be punctured. Fortunately repairs are fairly easy (see page 123) once you have located and exposed the damage.

Butyl comes in various thicknesses and qualities, something to bear in mind when comparing costs. Some of the cheaper butyl liners have less flexibility and tear resistance, but are much closer to the price of PVC liners and still have most of the merits of butyl.

If you are planning a very large pond, which means sheets will have been joined, make sure the joints are vulcanised. Strip joins are satisfactory for repairs but not for the basic construction.

Concrete Included only for completeness, not because a concrete pond is to be recommended. They can be very pleasant visually, and they may last a lifetime, but they involve a considerable amount of hard construction work, and more importantly it must be done properly if the pond is to last. You simply cannot afford to take short-cuts. Poorly constructed, you may find cracks or leaks in a year or two, which are difficult to repair, and are often solved by using a liner anyway.

Glass-fibre (glass-reinforced plastic) Expensive, but not to be dismissed if you want a pre-formed pool. Glass-fibre pools are virtually indestructible in normal use, and should last a gardening lifetime if treated with respect. Only two things are likely to deter you from this choice: cost

1) To lay brickwork to a curve, stretch the measure from a central peg to mark the radius.

2) Lay the bedding mortar to the line scribed by the trowel.

3) Position each brick so that it follows the curve, and check levels constantly.

A raised pool should be a full brick width (the width of two bricks side by side).

If using a liner in a raised pond you should be able to finish it off by taking it in at the required course of bricks.

Unless a liner is being used, a raised pool will need adequate foundations and base before the brickwork is built up.

A raised pool, sealed with a waterproof paint.

and the limitations of size and shape (a problem with all pre-formed pools).

Do not be tempted by intricate shapes with narrow waists: these may look all right in plan view, but viewed at an angle in the ground seem somehow less satisfactory, and often mean in proportions. You will also need to bear in mind that not all the designers of these pools are gardeners, and things like marginal shelves can be inadequate in amount or depth. Unless you want the pool for raising fry or simply to provide a small pool of water to attract wildlife, you will need to look at the largest sizes. Even some of these lack the depth and area desirable for a well-balanced pool.

Plastic, vacuum-formed An inexpensive alternative to glass-fibre pools. They are likely to have a better depth, but you cannot expect them to last as long; they will be more vulnerable to damage and you cannot easily repair them.

Although not the answer for the serious pond enthusiast, pre-formed plastic pools have a useful role as breeding quarters for particular fish, for rearing fry, and as a nature pond for the children, where they can hatch frog and toad spawn, and generally learn about the creatures that will inevitably find their way there.

Polythene Not a serious contender for anything other than a temporary pond, perhaps for raising fry or as quarantine quarters. Use 500 gauge if possible (it is available in an opaque blue if you prefer). Polythene should always be used double-thickness. Some firms offer two-sheet packs with one sheet clear and the other blue; you place the blue on top of the clear. Always fit a polythene liner in the excavation before running in the water (with other materials you let the weight of the water carry the liner into the hole).

PVC Laminated PVC liners are very popular. They are unaffected by frost, have a reasonable life expectancy (they should be all right for 10 years or more) and are cheaper than most other proper pond liners.

PVC liners do not stretch in the same way as butyl, so they do not contour quite so well into awkward shapes; but

you should have little trouble provided that you realise that there will inevitably be wrinkles. Those at the bottom will certainly not be noticed once the pond has been established for a month or two and the floor covered with the debris of pond life.

The big drawback to liners of this kind is their colour: usually blue or 'stone' (normally a buff shade). Perhaps it is the idea of blue-tiled swimming pools that makes blue an attractive colour for many people: images of crystal-clear water sparkling above a blue background. Unfortunately a pond is not like a swimming pool, and things happen to change the image. First the bottom and probably the sloping sides will become covered with soil and pond debris so that you will not see your fish against a blue background but against a black, muddy backcloth. Algae will probably grow on the sloping sides and look green and slimy. The part that will remain bright and shining blue will be any parts above water-level. Any shortcomings in construction, or drop of water level, will be all to obvious.

A more neutral stone colour is a little better, but still not as good as a black liner for avoiding offence to the eye.

Reinforced PVC These liners are like the above, but with nylon or terylene reinforcement between the laminations, providing extra strength. You can expect a life of at least 10 years.

The reinforcement gives the liner greater burst strength, but once the liner is in position between ground and water, that kind of strength is not going to be of great advantage. The reinforcement is unlikely to protect the liner from the sort of spearing accident that sometimes happens. It is therefore worth questioning whether the reinforcement is worth the substantial extra cost.

COST

It is always difficult to give costs in a book; the prices will be out of date even before publication, and there is no substitute for checking current prices in catalogues and at garden centres.

As a starting point, it is possible to give an approximate guide to *comparative* costs (although there are bound to be wide variations between manufacturers). In the following table the measurements are based on a pond about 2.4 m × 1.5m × 45 cm (8 × 5 × 1½ ft). You are unlikely to find a pre-formed plastic pool of this size, and the comparative cost for that has been extrapolated from comparable sizes of smaller glass-fibre and plastic pools. With the exception of the polythene, the prices have been based on pools supplied by one major supplier of water garden equipment, but you may find a wide price variation with other makes. A two-sheet polythene liner can be nearly four times more expensive from one firm than from another; but quality and thickness (not always made clear) should be taken into account. As the most expensive polythene sold as a pond liner brings the cost quite close to PVC, which has much

longer life and better appearance, you would probably only use an inexpensive polythene liner for a temporary pool. The prices below have therefore been calculated using a polythene pond liner pack offered by a major polythene supplier as the base against which other liner prices have been calculated in this table.

Material	Cost index*
Polythene (double thickness)	1
Laminated PVC	4
Economy quality butyl	6
Laminated PVC with nylon reinforcement	7.5
Butyl (0.03 in)	8
Concrete	10
Rigid plastic**	10
Butyl with stone-coloured plastic laminate	13
Glass-fibre	21

*The base price is taken as a two-sheet polythene pond liner kit supplied by a plastics specialist. You can expect an economy quality butyl to cost six times as much, a laminated PVC liner about four times as much. The relative prices may change if larger sheets are needed.
**You are unlikely to find rigid plastic pools of the dimensions compared.

MAKING A POOL WITH A LINER

1) Mark the area out on the ground. Use a long piece of rope or a hose-pipe (if the

weather is warm and the hose supple) to mark the outline. You could sprinkle sand or something similar on the ground to achieve the same effect, but this is much less easy to adjust if you do not get it right the first time.

Start removing a shallow area of soil a few inches deep within the area marked by the rope or hose-pipe, then double-check that shape and size is satisfactory before proceeding.

2) Excavate the soil to the required depth, leaving marginal shelves about 23 cm (9 in) below water-level. All side walls should have a slope of about 20 degrees. If setting the pool into a lawn, use planks between the pond and the lawn edge so that the loaded wheelbarrow does not damage the grass. Cut back the edges sufficiently to take any paving that is to edge the pond.

3) Insert wooden pegs about 1 m (3 – 4 ft) apart around the edge of the pool, and use a spirit-level (or spirit-level and straight-edge) to check that the ground is level. If possible, also measure from a long peg in the centre of the pool to pegs around the edge too. This job is the one most likely to be skipped or rushed, yet it will make a vital difference to the finished pond. Once the water is in, any error in levelling will be very obvious, so be patient at this stage.

4) Check that all surfaces are smooth and free of protruding stones (make sure there are no tree roots, though you should not be making a pond close to a tree), then line the excavation with a 12 mm (½ in) layer of damp sand (dry sand will not cling to the sides). A thick layer of damp newspapers could be used instead of sand. If the ground is very stony, however, it is worth using polyester matting as well as sand or newspaper. This will not decay, and you usually order it by the yard from a water garden specialist.

5) Drape the liner loosely into the excavation, but hold the edges down with bricks. Then start running in the water. As the pool fills the bricks can be eased off periodically to let the liner take up the contours of the hole. You are bound to get some creasing of the liner, although the worst can usually be removed by moving or stretching the liner a little as the pond fills.

6) Once the final water-level has been reached, trim off excess liner, leaving about 10 – 15 cm (4 – 6 in) on all round. If necessary, the edge can be kept in position temporarily with bricks or large nails pushed through the liner and into the ground at the edge of the flap.

7) If finishing with paving, lay the slabs on a bed of mortar, using three parts sand to one part cement. Bear in mind that paving should overlap the water by about 5 cm (2 in) for a neat finish. However, this could be unstable if small pieces of crazy-paving are used, so either use normal paving slabs or make sure large pieces are used at the pond edge if crazy-paving is laid. If much mortar drops into water while laying the edge, empty the water out and refill. If you have to lay cables into the pool (for a fountain for instance), make sure this is done before

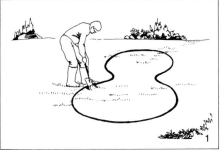

1

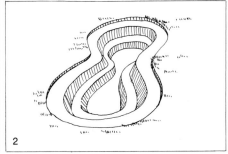

2

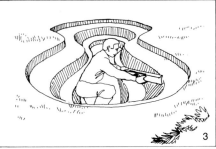

3

4

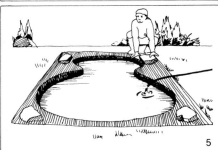

5

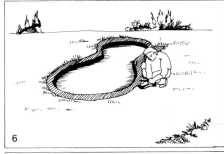

6

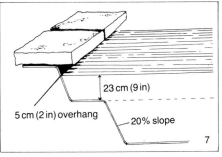

23 cm (9 in)

5 cm (2 in) overhang

20% slope

7

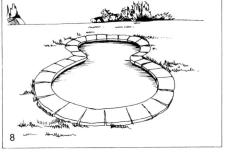

8

1

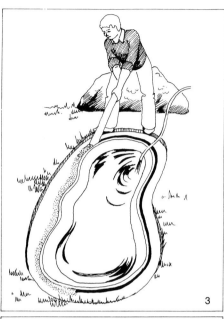

3

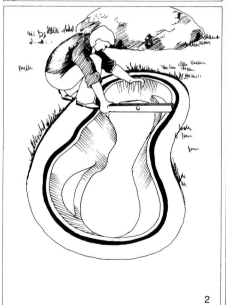

2

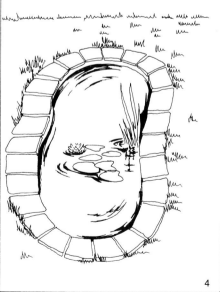

4

you lay the paving, otherwise you will have to run the wire over the paving, a constant reminder of lack of forethought.

INSTALLING A PRE-FORMED POOL

A pre-formed pool sounds easy to install, but getting the level right is just as difficult, and just as important, as with a liner. It is so easy to think that it looks level, only to find that when filled with water you have a few inches of plastic (or glass-fibre) showing at one side.

1) Excavate a hole the same shape as the pool, but about 15 cm (6 in) wider all round. If you try to excavate a hole to the exact dimensions you are almost doomed to failure. If there are intricate shelves and contours it is easier to excavate whole areas to the full depth. You may have to allow for the edging or lip. One with a simulated rock or crazy-paving edge will have a wider flange than one with a plain edge. If you have to pave over the flange, allow for the depth of the paving.

2) Make sure the bottom of the hole is well compacted and level, then spread 2.5 cm (1 in) of sand over the base of the excavation. Place the pool in the hole to test for size. Even if the depth seems right, take it out again and look at the impression on the sand. The pool must be fully supported on the base, so, if it appears that there are pockets that are too shallow, fill with more sand. Use a straight-edge and spirit-level to make sure the pool is level in all directions.

3) Once the pool is level, start filling the pool with water and back-filling around the outside with sand and sifted soil. Glass-fibre pools can be filled first, then back-filled, but semi-rigid pools should be filled and compacted at the same time (a method that you can also use for glass-fibre pools). Use a stout piece of timber to ram the soil and sand down the sides and beneath any shelves (pay particular attention to this point). Try to keep the back-filling level with the water in the pool. Stop periodically to check levels. If levels are suffering as a result of back-filling you can correct them easily at this stage, but it is a major job if you wait.

4) Edge with paving or rocks, or whatever other finish is suitable, but empty and refill the pool again if you drop much mortar into the water while doing this.

MAKING A CONCRETE POND

As you are likely to be a handyman to tackle this, step-by-step instructions are not included, but see the illustration on p. 38. The reinforcement is important.

Keep to a design that is simple: not too many curves and bays, no very steep walls (aim for a slope of 20 degrees).

A waterproofing compound can be added at the dry mix stage.

You will probably need to use shuttering, but make sure this is greased or soaked beforehand so that the concrete does not stick to the wood as it sets. In hot weather, cover the exposed concrete with wet sacks so that it does not dry out too quickly.

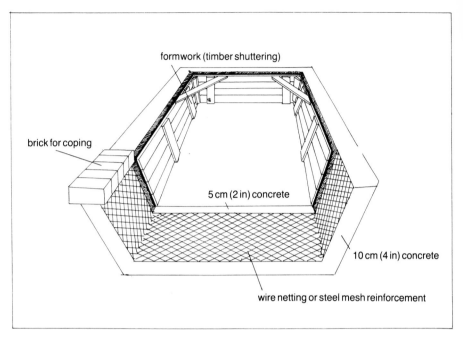

formwork (timber shuttering)

brick for coping

5 cm (2 in) concrete

10 cm (4 in) concrete

wire netting or steel mesh reinforcement

A concrete pool needs reinforcement for strength. Formwork may be needed to form the sides.

Having made the pool, even more patience is needed. The free lime has to be eliminated before it is safe for plants and fish. If you want to wait six months, nature will do all the necessary work for you; most of us want more instant results.

You can empty and refill the pool several times and hope that it is then safe, but it is generally easier to paint on a neutralising agent. You could simply use household vinegar (one part vinegar to ten parts water), and scrub the concrete with this, giving the pond a change of water afterwards. Better is a proprietary neutralising preparation that you mix with water and paint on. This not only neutralises the lime but also seals the concrete.

There are also liquid plastic and chlorinated rubber paints that you can use on your concrete pond, but these are generally used after repairs.

MAKING A RAISED POND

A pool does not have to be raised very high to be effective. Even if it comes only 23 – 30 cm (9 – 12 in) above the surrounding paving, a formal pool can still look interesting.

Once you decide on a raised pool of any

A beach edge of cobbles or pebbles is a good way to deal with a liner pond so that it looks neat.

kind, it has to be constructed as a raised pool even if most of it is below ground. Having much of the water below ground level means that you have the worst of both worlds in terms of construction: you still have a lot of excavating, plus the work involved in constructing a raised pond.

It is not possible, in the limited space of a book of this size, to explain brick-laying techniques in detail, and you may have to consult a garden construction book if you are uncertain about laying foundations and laying bricks.

The illustration on p. 40 shows the basic principles of making a raised pond. Bricks are shown here, but you could use building blocks instead, especially if you plan to use a liner in the pool.

Keep to a simple bond such as an English bond, as strength is more important than a fancy pattern. The top row is best finished with bricks laid side by side. Curved raised ponds are always impressive, but are perhaps for the more experienced bricklayer. You must lay to a carefully marked radius by using a string attached to a peg in the centre of the area scribing the laying line in the mortar bed with a pointing trowel.

Let the concrete foundation set for a couple of days before attempting to lay the bricks.

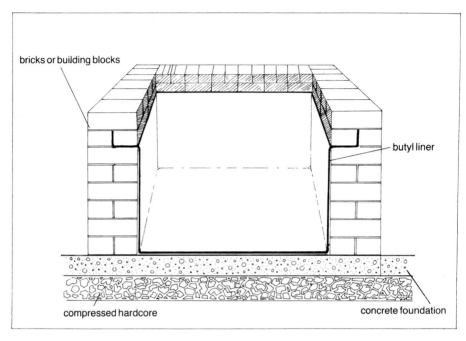

bricks or building blocks

butyl liner

compressed hardcore

concrete foundation

A liner can also be used for a raised pool. It will have to be pleated in the corners in a formal shape like this.

The mortar joints on the inside should be flush and smooth, and the whole pond will have to be treated with a water-proofing compound. These can be liquid plastic or chlorinated rubber paints. You may need to use a primer, so check the instructions carefully.

A butyl liner (being black it is hardly noticeable) is an even surer method of making it waterproof. Fold the end in between the brickwork a couple of courses from the top, where you want the water level to finish (see illustration). You can use a liner on rectangular and circular raised pools; in the case of a pool with right-angled corners you will have to pleat the liner. Certainly there will be some creases, but you are unlikely to find these noticeable once filled with water.

FINISHING THE EDGES

The majority of ponds are paved at the edge. Natural stone always looks best, of course, but even that surrounding a pond can make it look too artificial. Sometimes a more natural finish is called for.

Getting a natural effect with grass to the edge is very difficult; the soil tends to wash into the water and then expose the liner. If you want to try grass to the edge,

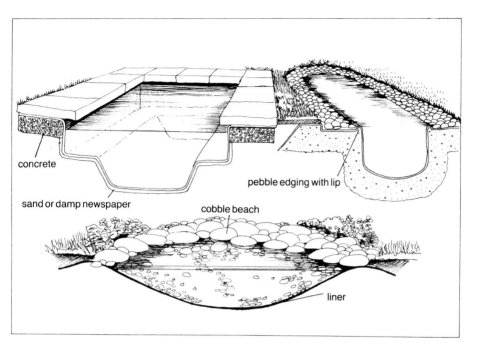

concrete

sand or damp newspaper

pebble edging with lip

cobble beach

liner

Perhaps the most difficult part of constructing a pond with a liner is getting the edges neat so that the liner does not show. Here are three suggestions for coping with the problem. None of these will be successful if the pond is not level of course, so you must still check levels constantly during construction.

extend the liner to make a very gradual slope beneath the grass and let turves overlap the liner slightly.

Pebble or cobble beaches provide another solution. Again the pond must have a very gradual slope at the edge to avoid the pebbles rolling down and exposing the liner. Make sure the beach starts below the water line and extend it well out of the water too.

If using paving, make sure the slabs overlap the edge of the water by an inch or two: this will give a crisper line to the pond, and reduce the chances of the liner looking obtrusive if the water level drops a bit.

4·INTERESTING FEATURES

If your prime interest is in providing a home for fish and aquatic plants, there is little point in making life difficult by making a pond some complicated shape, or incorporating some sophisticated water feature.

Water offers opportunities far beyond the kidney-shaped pool or a formal rec-

tangular sunken pond, however, and if you want to make water a more positive feature in the garden design it might be worth thinking about some of the other water and associated features that you could incorporate.

STREAMS AND RILLS

The suggestion of a stream in a small

A small raised pool, bringing the life of the pond nearer eye level.

A raised pond. One of the waterlilies is a tropical lily put outdoors for the summer.

garden, or perhaps a larger garden in a town, might sound either ridiculous or pretentious. Even in a more natural setting the prospect of creating a stream might seem formidable. Obviously the flow will have to be created by a pump, and the scale modest, but the project is certainly practical.

There are constraints. A 'stream' will provide a wonderful setting for plants, but the scope for fish-keeping will be severely limited. A man-made stream say 30 cm (1 ft) deep will not be suitable for large fish. Ideas of fish the size of trout

sometimes found in natural streams of that size should be dismissed: in nature there is a constant flow of fresh water, and probably deeper areas where the fish can take refuge when necessary. In your back-garden stream the same water is simply being re-circulated and with such a shallow depth it will heat up excessively in summer, and freeze more easily in winter. It may even freeze solid.

Green water is also likely to be a particular problem, because the shallow depth will mean that from spring onwards the water will become warm and the sunlight will easily penetrate most of the depth – ideal conditions for the growth of algae.

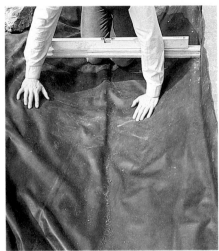

Although ponds are more popular, a long, narrow 'stream' can make an interesting feature too. Something as shallow as this will be suitable for only small fish, and will look best linked with a larger pool.

Here the hose for the fountain is being laid before the liner is put in position.

Getting the edges level is just as important with a shallow 'stream' as with a normal pond.

There are some solutions: you can opt for no fish and water plants, and keep the water sparkling clear the year round with the aid of chemicals; or you can link the stream with a deeper pond with which the water is circulated, and keep only very small fish in the stream (assuming that the pond and the stream are not continuous; if they are you will have few problems anyway).

You will find butyl rubber one of the best materials for making a water course like this (see step-by-step guide below). You could use other liners, but the black finish will make any creases less obvious

and, although it is only an illusion, increase the apparent depth of water.

If you find that some of the small fish are not very noticeable against the dark background, a layer of white gravel over the bottom can look attractive and help to display the fish. The effect is soon lost of course unless you are prepared to rake out fallen leaves and other debris occasionally.

Making a stream
1) Excavate the area, making sure the sides slope naturally, and remove any protruding stones or tree or shrub roots.
2) Lay the hose for the fountain or cascade. You could take out a deeper channel for this, but it should not be necessary as the outline of the hose

44

Running in the water. The edges are not trimmed until the water finds its own level and you know that no more adjustments are necessary.

Finally the surplus liner can be trimmed.

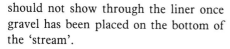

should not show through the liner once gravel has been placed on the bottom of the 'stream'.

3) Check levels along the whole length, then place the liner over the excavation. Run in the water, and check levels again.

4) Trim off excess liner, tucking it beneath the edging paving if possible, or edge with rocks.

Rills There are some gardens in which something more formal is called for, and a rill, perhaps across a patio, is a possibility. This is a far more ambitious project because you will have to sink chambers into the ground to provide a reservoir of water, and the whole system

is much more difficult to make leakproof, especially if you are depending on concrete seals. It is worth using a liner too, and to lay your bricks over this if you have doubts about making a good job of waterproofing the concrete.

This use of water, which depends purely on the sight and sound of shallow running water for its effect, obviously has to be kept clean. Chemicals can be used to prevent the growth of algae and other organisms, but you will also have to use filters to keep leaves and debris out of the reservoir.

Evaporation will be a problem too in the summer, especially if the water depth is perhaps only an inch. For that reason you will need to install a permanent water supply with a ball valve to keep the reservoir topped up.

45

RAISED PONDS

Raised ponds (construction methods are described on pp. 38 – 40) can be simple or complex. If you are going to have a raised pond, there is a lot to be said for making a bold feature of it, perhaps by having several linking sections with cascades from one to the other. This approach needs a suitable setting of course, but the actual treatment of the pools can also affect their suitability for a particular position.

A series of say three linking raised pools, like the one illustrated below, might look perfectly acceptable on a formal patio or in some other setting where simplicity of line is important. Plants and fish may be considered unnecessary; the water says it all.

You could, however, change the whole atmosphere and tone by making them fairly shallow and using suitable rocks and water plants with perhaps spiky or otherwise suitably 'architectural' leaves. This will probably make this otherwise very artificial use of water perfectly acceptable even in a plantsman's garden.

Stepped formal pools create a lot of sound and movement from the fountain and cascades.

BOG GARDENS

The concept of a bog garden sounds attractive: bold drifts of those moisture-loving plants that are often difficult to grow well normally, acting as a backdrop for the pond itself.

A moment's reflection will reveal that a bog garden needs a fair degree of thought if it is to be successful. It is no use adding some peat into the surrounding soil and hoping that the plants will thrive. If you have made your

An informal pond with extensive bog garden.

pond leak-proof the soil an inch from the edge will be as dry as the soil in the rest of the garden. Adding lots of peat may only make matters worse once it dries out, because it will be difficult to rewet.

There are plenty of ordinary garden plants that *associate* well with water, hostas and astilbes for instance, and you can use these very effectively without going to the trouble of making a proper bog garden. There are some plants, however, that really do need boggy ground that rarely dries, and for these you will have to make special provision.

If you are making a pool with a liner, you can just extend an area at the edge of

the pool to provide a broad, shallow ledge the size of the bog garden about 30 cm (1 ft) deep. The boundary between bog garden and pool will have to be made with rows of bricks or blocks to keep the soil (ideally equal parts peat and clay soil) contained. Place a thick layer of gravel in the bottom of the bog, then pile up the soil so that it is banked up, at least 15 cm (6 in) and preferably 30 cm (1 ft) above the water level. Bog plants are not aquatics and the roots should only be in waterlogged conditions for brief periods. The soil should be high enough above the water level to receive water by capillary action, not by direct contact.

There is a problem with this 'integrated' approach. Unless you are careful the water in the pond can become very muddy, and unless your retaining wall is firm and secure you might find a very messy situation in a year or two if it begins to weaken.

A bog fed directly by the pond should never be too large in relation to the pond itself (about 10 per cent of the area is enough), not because more would *look* wrong, but because it could seriously affect the water level in the pond. Evaporation over the additional shallow area, and the extra moisture taken up by the bog plants will all influence the water level in the pond itself.

If you are installing a pre-formed or concrete pool, or the pond is already built, then of course the integrated bog garden is no longer open to you and you will have to build a separate bog garden and try to merge it as best you can with the pond. The simplest way is still a liner, covering a shallow depression about 18 cm (1½ ft) deep, with the soil banked well above liner level. There are no masking problems at the edge of the liner because you can cut it off a few inches below normal soil level. It does not have to be a watertight liner either, and you could use an old pond liner that has sprung a leak; or simply use polythene, as there is no point in going to great expense when it is not necessary. Make some slits in the liner about 15 cm (6 in) below normal soil level to provide drainage and prevent waterlogging in very heavy rain. Again, bank the soil up slightly above the surrounding ground so that the roots do not sit in waterlogged soil, but because the ground will not need to be raised so much it can be more natural and pleasing.

It is sometimes recommended that such bog gardens are placed so that the pond can be flooded to overflow into the bog garden periodically. This is not a satisfactory arrangement; it means remembering to do it, and of course adding cold water to the pond unnecessarily. It is more satisfactory to bury a PVC hosepipe in the bed as you fill it, leaving one end exposed so that you can connect a hose-pipe periodically during the summer. If you do this, make sure the end of the hose-pipe is capped off, pierce small holes along the length of the part to be buried, and use a push-on connector at the exposed end to make coupling a quick and easy job.

A final word of caution if you are still

undecided about a bog garden: give it a miss if you are not prepared to give it regular attention during the summer. Any bog garden will provide a superb seed-bed for weed seeds, which will flourish as well as most bog plants. Unless you have a bog that is fed directly from the main pond it will be essential to keep the bog irrigated during hot, dry spells in summer. Although dry soil will check most plants, it can spell disaster for true bog plants.

BUBBLE FOUNTAINS AND FOUNTAIN ORNAMENTS

If bog gardens sound a bit of a bother, something more simple like a bubble fountain might appeal. There are many different forms of bubble fountains (not to be confused with a geyser, used as a form of fountain within a pond; see page 61), and a range of them are illustrated

throughout the book. They can be simple or sophisticated, but above all they are one of the safest water features if you have small children to worry about. They are likely to appeal even to those for whom a 'real' water feature is not a serious contender, but they can contribute so much to the design of a garden that even the dedicated pond enthusiast ought to consider them as an *additional* appealing use of water in the garden.

Both bubble fountains and some of the Mediterranean style self-contained fountains (illustrated on p. 50) look most at home on a patio, although sometimes they can help to brighten up an otherwise uninteresting corner of the garden. Some of the larger or more ornate free-standing and self-contained fountains can look pretentious unless you have just the right

You can buy kits that contain all you need for a super bubble fountain. No need to search round for a genuine millstone − glass-fibre achieves the same effect and is a lot lighter to handle!

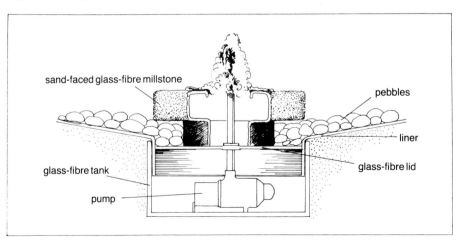

49

A bubble fountain like this will be quite expensive, but can be a dominant focal point.

A plain pool will benefit from a statue or ornament as a centrepiece.

setting. They have the advantage of needing nothing more than topping up with water and the provision of a small pump. They are heavy to manhandle into position, however, and do not imagine that these are a cheap option for a water feature: they can cost several times the price of a respectably-sized pool made with a liner.

BARRELS AND OTHER TUBS

A half-barrel will make a charming miniature water garden if you can make it watertight. Make sure the hoops are in good condition and if necessary soak the barrel for a week (if you already have a pond, this is an ideal place to soak it, after first scrubbing it out).

A half-barrel pool. The waterlily is 'Froebeli'.

Sometimes soaking will not stop all the leaks, but if you make a note of where the water is leaking, then empty the barrel and dry the area; a black mastic will usually make it watertight again.

Much more readily available are plastic shrub tubs of various kinds, including rectangular ones, that do not have drainage holes already punched in them. These can be filled with water and planted immediately.

Ideal for a patio, these miniature water gardens can be great fun. They will take a waterlily (but you must choose a suitably small species), and a couple of other water plants. You can even have a few small fish to add interest, although these are best overwintered in a larger pond or indoors, as a raised container like this can freeze solid in a severe winter.

You could always sink the containers into the ground (in which case the problem of winter protection for small fish will not be necessary).

5·FOUNTAINS AND CASCADES

If there is one thing more appealing than a sheet of clear water, it is the sound and sight of moving water. Whether it is the natural appearance of a well-constructed cascade (waterfall if you prefer, though this implies something rather grand), or the very contrived fountain so beloved by pond owners, the constantly changing music of water on water and the ever-changing patterns of the surface seldom fail to attract.

Splashing water is welcomed by fish too. To a limited extent it helps to oxygenate the water, but more importantly the turbulence helps to speed up the release of carbon dioxide from the water. This is a good thing at any time, but during hot summer weather it can mean the difference between life and death for some fish, particularly golden orfe, which need well-oxygenated water.

Because fountains and cascades are both useful and attractive in their own right does not mean that a combination of both will be best. On the contrary, a setting that is right for a cascade is unlikely to be right for a fountain. Generally, fountains are best in formal pools, cascades in 'natural' pools. Water might of course cascade effectively over a lip in interlinked formal pools, but then if you had a fountain too one would almost certainly detract from the other.

If you want to incorporate both (and many pumps have both a cascade pipe and a fountain head), try to arrange them at opposite ends of the pond. Ask yourself first whether the impact would not be better with just one.

A spectacular type of fountain known as a water sphere. Bear in mind that this type is far from attractive when the pump is switched off!

EQUIPMENT

Getting cascades and fountains to work effectively, and to look right, is

52

This type of fountain is known as a water bell.

unfortunately not a foregone conclusion. Keeping a sense of scale and proportion is one part of the formula for success, getting the right pumps and equipment is the other. On this latter point there is much to be said for consulting a specialist water garden supplier for advice on what you need for your garden. General principles are outlined in this chapter, but it

is impossible to cover all the different needs, and the pumps available and their performance may also change. You may also want to make your decisions armed with the precise costs of the various options.

If you go to a specialist with all the relevant dimensions, including the total lift (maximum height the water has to be lifted to), and the width of sills, and explain what you want to achieve, he

In design terms a water spout can be just as effective as a torrent of water over a cascade, and you can manage with a much more modest pump.

should be able to advise you on a selection of the most suitable equipment.

Priorities are different for fountains and cascades. Volume rather than pressure is the key factor for a cascade, but for a fountain pressure is more important.

You will almost certainly be tempted by the simplicity of a submersible pump; surface pumps require the construction of a special chamber and much more plumbing.

Submersible pumps should present few problems and you can have one working within half an hour of opening the box. There are both mains and low voltage systems. The low voltage systems are likely to operate at 24 volts from a transformer inside the house or garage.

Unless the pool is immediately outside the house, you will have to connect the pump lead to an extension lead. Connect the two with a weatherproof connector (a good water garden specialist should be able to supply this), and cover the connector with a paving slab or something similar. You will need to take the pump indoors for the winter, and you can just disconnect it at this point. For a low-voltage system the extension cable will be wired into the transformer. For a mains voltage pump it will have to be connected to an earthed electrical point, and it is

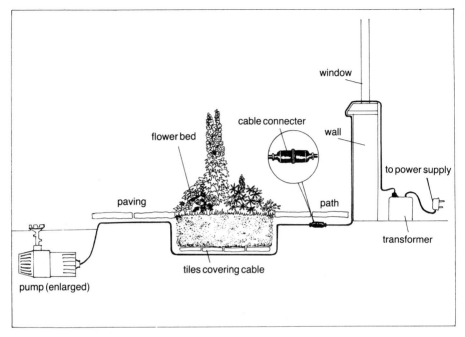

window

cable connecter

wall

flower bed

to power supply

paving

path

transformer

tiles covering cable

pump (enlarged)

most advisable to have it on a circuit protected by an earth leakage circuit breaker (sometimes known as a residual current device). If the circuit is not protected, you can buy special plugs that incorporate the device; but they are of course much more expensive than ordinary plugs.

The submersible pump itself is best stood on a couple of bricks to keep the inlet clear of the debris on the bottom of the pond.

Surface pumps are unnecessary for a fountain or cascade of modest size, but you will have to consider one of these if a relatively high head is required for a waterfall or fountain, or where the one

A low-voltage submersible pump is particularly easy to install, and perfectly adequate for a small pond. However, you will need a more powerful pump if you want a large waterfall or fountain.

pump is to power several fountains. These pumps are not really much more expensive than comparable submersibles, but you will certainly incur additional costs in providing the necessary chamber and plumbing. They must be housed in a properly constructed, dry and well ventilated chamber. If sunken, it ought to be brick lined and have a proper inspection cover, and there should be no chance of surface water entering it and flooding it. The pump itself should be supported off the floor, which should have drainage holes. The chamber must be large

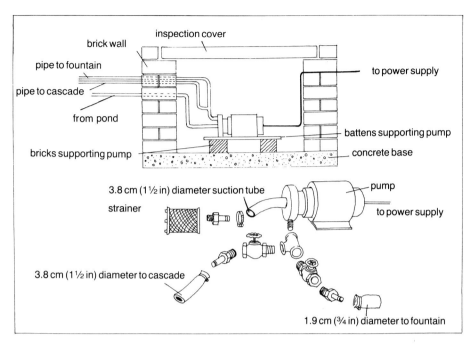

brick wall
inspection cover
pipe to fountain
pipe to cascade
from pond
to power supply
bricks supporting pump
battens supporting pump
concrete base

3.8 cm (1 ½ in) diameter suction tube
pump
strainer
to power supply

3.8 cm (1 ½ in) diameter to cascade

1.9 cm (¾ in) diameter to fountain

A surface pump is quite difficult to install properly, and it is best to ask the advice of a specialist supplier of water garden equipment, who will advise on the various fittings as well as the most suitable type and capacity of pump.

enough not only to take the pump, but also the associated pipework (without acute bends), valves and stopcocks.

If the pump is below water level, you will only need to use a strainer as the pump will be kept primed by gravity, but a pump housed above water level will also need a footvalve strainer (an off-putting term but a water garden specialist will know what you want).

If you intend to run the pump for only short periods of say a few hours at a time, then either series wound or induction

motors can be used, but for continuous running you need an induction type motor. Some induction motors should have a starter with a thermal overload trip, and installation becomes a job for an electrician unless you are sure of what you are doing.

The pump should be positioned to keep the suction hose as short as possible.

Do not buy any accessories and tubing until you know which pump you are going to buy. The size of the tubes will depend on the pump and may vary from say ⅝ in to 2 in (16–50mm) diameter. Suction pipes from pond to external pump may need to be especially strong to prevent them collapsing under the suction (which would restrict flow and

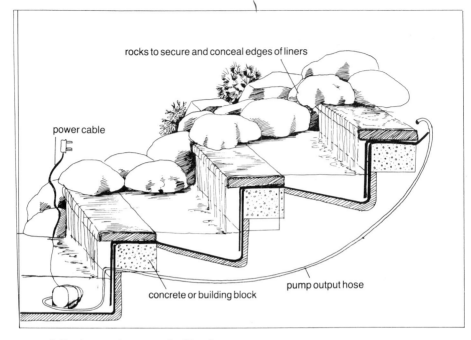

rocks to secure and conceal edges of liners

power cable

concrete or building block

pump output hose

potentially harm the pump). For long runs of hose, it may be necessary to increase the diameter to compensate for friction. Let the specialist supplier who provides the pump advise you on these points.

MAKING A CASCADE

The easiest way is to buy a set of glass-fibre (glass-reinforced plastic) or heavy-duty moulded polythene cascade trays and to set them in a bank with each lip overlapping the tray beneath. The glass-fibre trays have a rough finish, the poly-thene trays a smooth finish. Very occasionally this can work well, but

Cascades are quite difficult to construct without leaks and with an even flow of water over the lips. Make sure you have a pump large enough to generate the required flow of water.

usually the result looks like trays set in a bank. The problems are twofold: it is not easy to disguise the trays, and unless you have a natural slope the mound of soil into which they are set is likely to look far from convincing.

An ideal location for a cascade for an informal pool is a background rock garden, where a 'stream' and cascades tumble down among the rocks into the stream beneath. If this ideal does not exist, keep the steps fairly shallow; water dropping just a few inches will be enough to provide the necessary sounds.

58

A lion's mask ornament – the hose from a low-powered pump is simply pushed onto the pipe set into the back of the ornament.

You could make a concrete water course for your cascades, but this is hard work and prone to problems. A liner is likely to be a lot less trouble. Butyl rubber is the best choice because its flexibility and 'stretch' help it to conform to the contours more easily.

The illustrations below show the principles of construction, but there are a few

For many people, the 'mountain stream' type of waterfall is still the best form of moving water.

This type of rock pool looks impressive, but is very difficult to construct, especially as the weight of the rocks makes even minor adjustments hard work.

essential points to bear in mind. Make sure that the liner comes above the anticipated water level, and that at least 10 cm (4 in) of water remains in each 'dish' when the pump is switched off.

There are two principal methods of creating the necessary water turbulence at the lip. You can either fix a flat stone at the edge so that the water trickles or cascades over the lip, preferably with an overhang, or let the water surge through a row of rocks.

It will make the feature more interesting, and emphasise the movement of the water, if you can break up the surface by suitably placed rocks within each tier. If you are worried about the rocks damaging the liner, either set them in concrete or bed them on a thick layer of gravel. Treat cement surfaces with a neutralising agent before filling with water.

The width of the lip, and the strength of flow that you require (trickle or fast flow) will also dictate the power of the pump you require. As a guide, most of the preformed cascade trays will need a flow of 250 gallons an hour. If you are making a cascade from a liner, a flow of 300 gallons an hour will produce a thin, continuous sheet of water about 15 cm (6 in) wide. For a wider or more vigorous flow you will need a bigger pump. You can get some idea of the output required for a modest cascade by running a hose into the cascade and increasing the volume until the required cascade is achieved. You can then run the hose into a suitable container for one minute and measure how many pints it has delivered. Multiplying the answer by 7.5 will give the number of gallons in an hour. For the flow in litres, simply measure in litres and multiply by 60. A good supplier should be able to tell you the output for a particular pump for a given head (height to which the water has to be pumped).

FOUNTAINS

If your pond and your purse are big enough, you can indulge in very elaborate fountains with a range of intricate patterns, illuminated with lights that change colour if you want. For most people, the range of simple fountain heads that come with most submersible pumps will be perfectly adequate. You can usually vary the spray pattern and spread. The spread can be particularly important for a small pool as a display that constantly lets the spray drift away from the pool will result in a significant water loss.

You can buy fountains that change the pattern automatically every 12-16 seconds. Although this may be an unnecessary refinement in an informal pool, in a formal pool, perhaps in a patio setting, it will add considerably to the interest and make the fountain even more of a focal point.

Make sure the fountain head is above the water. This may mean standing the pump on bricks.

Bell fountains throw out a dome-like sheet of water from a nozzle that protrudes from the surface. These are very attractive in a formal setting, and some of the more elaborate ones, such as those with three heads can look very 'architectural'. Although more gimmicky, you can even buy water bell fountains that spray mini-jets of water within the bell.

Geysers combine air with a low but broad spout of water, creating a foaming, bubbling effect. They need a fairly powerful pump, and the combination of this type of fountain and the pump can work out quite expensive; but the result can be impressive, especially if you arrange some rocks around the geyser so that it bubbles up from the rocks and over them. Generally, however, you need a fairly large expanse of water as a geyser could be too dominant and disruptive in a small pond.

Gargoyles and masks have little place in an informal pond, but in a formal setting they can add just the right touch of distinction. They are ideal where a semi-circular pond adjoins a wall, or even as a bubble fountain in reverse on say a patio; the water can spout from the mask and tumble onto cobbles below to find its way to a reservoir for pumping back to the mask via a pipe built into the wall. The same problems of evaporation and splash losses face this as a bubble fountain, so make sure that the reservoir is kept topped up.

Ornaments that spout water, such as herons, frogs and fish, for instance, *can* look good. They can also look rather hideous. They are probably on a par with gnomes; you either like them or hate

Low-voltage pond lighting is very easy to install. By weighting down the cable the lights can be submerged.

This is not the sort of display that you will get from normal amateur fountains and lighting kits, but it shows what can be achieved, and specialist firms will be able to advise you on this kind of display.

them, but sometimes even the dubious have to admit that they look good in a particular setting.

POND LIGHTING

Lighting has been included in this chapter because the best effect is usually achieved where the lights play onto moving water, creating shimmering rainbows of dancing light. Some fountains contain built-in lighting directed up at the jets; some of the more expensive ones have a revolving disc that changes the colour of the light automatically.

It is worth trying to see a particular lighting kit in use before you order. Some of the underwater and floating lights will probably be a disappointment unless they illuminate the water close to a fountain or the fall of a cascade. Even then you might not find the sight of the lamps beneath

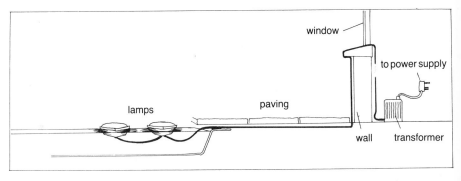

the surface acceptable during daylight. There is a lot to be said for buying lighting combined with the fountain if you want underwater lighting.

Above-surface lighting can be equally effective, possibly more so. The lamps need to be suitably hidden or screened of course, and they ought to play on a particularly attractive part of the pond, especially on moving water such as a fountain or cascade.

Unless you spend much more time outdoors in your garden after dusk than the average gardener, pond lights will probably be low on your list of priorities (they will probably be used less often than you imagine).

Some pond lights operate at 12 volts from a transformer sited indoors, but others use mains voltage. Be especially careful with mains voltage lights: it is essential that they are designed for use near or in water, and use an earth leakage circuit breaker (see page 56) for additional safety. Mains lights are likely to be more powerful, but the low-voltage lights are simple and safe, and if a bulb fails you can just replace it with a car headlight bulb with some systems.

Colours are usually easily altered by changing the lenses, but you may find the normal white light is the most effective.

Some low-voltage lighting systems are easily moved about (those designed for normal above-water use may have spikes at the base that you simply push into the ground). These can easily be moved around when different plants are in flower, so that something of interest is always picked out in light.

6·PLANTING THE POOL

Do not expect too much from your plants during the first season. They are not likely to look like the large, impressive clumps that you may have seen in established water gardens and in many of the illustrations in this book; although there are exceptions, it will be the second season before they look respectable, and the third before they look impressive. Like most plants, they need time to become established.

None of this should deter you, because every established pond was newly planted once. Just be cautious about the plants that you introduce: avoid the rampant ones that you will regret by the end of the first year (these have been indicated in the list of plants), and plant

Choose a variety of plants to suit the different levels. The planting depth (PD) is the distance between the top of the compost and the surface of the water, not from the base of the container.

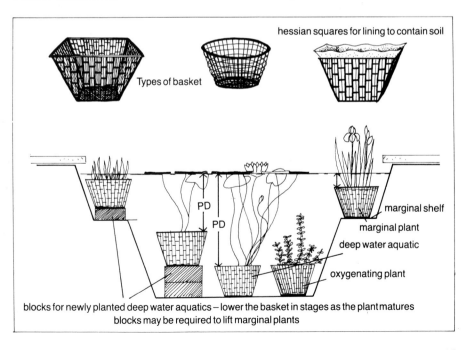

hessian squares for lining to contain soil

Types of basket

PD

PD

marginal shelf
marginal plant
deep water aquatic
oxygenating plant

blocks for newly planted deep water aquatics – lower the basket in stages as the plant matures
blocks may be required to lift marginal plants

those that really are going to be dependable and worth waiting for.

Any list of recommended plants must be subjective, and one person's idea of an attractive plant may not be the same as another's. However, to narrow the bewildering choice of possible plants that you could use, each entry in this chapter has been given a rating that should make it easier if you do not already know the plants.

Remember that you should think of planting in 'levels': some for the bottom of the pond, some on the shallower 'marginal shelf', some in marshy ground beside the pond (bog plants), and some to plant near the pond because they associate well with water though you can grow them without a pond (astilbes and hostas, for example). To make selection easier, the plants have been arranged in a similar way here.

PLANTING AQUATICS

Waterlilies are best planted in a bowl or similar shallow container. Use a heavy loam (water garden specialists usually sell suitable compost, though you would not want to order this by post). Avoid a rich compost, otherwise the excess fertiliser will encourage the growth of algae and contribute to green water. If applying a special waterlily fertiliser, sprinkle it over the compost. Some waterlily fertilisers come in a sachet that you bury in the compost.

Applying a waterlily fertiliser to the planting container – in this case a washing-up bowl.

Disturb the waterlily roots as little as possible, but make sure the roots are well firmed into the soil – which should preferably be a heavy loam. You can buy suitable soil from a water plant supplier.

Waterlilies are likely to be growing in a container when you buy them (sometimes they will be sold without soil). Remove the container before planting. Place just one waterlily in the centre of each container.

Submerged oxygenated plants are likely to be sold as cutting or small plants. These may be sold as a collection wrapped in a container sealed with transparent film. Do not open them until ready to plant.

Oxygenating plants are usually planted in separate containers, but some can be put round the edge of containers used for larger plants. To help anchor the plants, and to reduce the chance of fish stirring up mud, dress the top of the container with gravel.

Water the container before submerging it. Otherwise the dry soil or compost will probably float about as you put the container in the water, causing muddy water. Deep-water aquatics such as waterlilies should be lowered to their full depth in stages. Stand the container on bricks initially, then remove these in stages as the plants grow.

The same principles of planting apply to other aquatic plants, though most of them will be grown in pots and it is more usual to use the open-mesh plastic baskets illustrated below instead of a solid container such as a washing-up bowl. You will have to buy liners for these baskets otherwise the soil will simply fall out. It is well worth using baskets like this rather than trying to grow your plants in pots, which will be

Oxygenators are often sold as collections, though you can of course buy individual plants.

If the container is large you can start some oxygenators off with the waterlilies, but it is often more convenient to keep them separate.

Topping the planting container with gravel will reduce the amount of mud produced when you put it in the water, and stop fish stirring up the soil.

Water the container thoroughly before placing in the pond. If the soil is dry when it is placed into the pond there may well be air pockets and fine soil particles will float and cloud the water.

unstable and probably topple over once there is a lot of top growth.

Generally it is better to plant only one type of plant to each container; then the weaker types will not suffer from competition from the more vigorous kinds.

For quicker effect you may want to plant several of the same kind in the one basket. As the baskets come in various sizes, it should not be difficult to choose ones to match the plants.

Do not be tempted to cover the base of the pond with soil for direct planting. You will have little control over the growth of the plants, and after a year or two the more rampant species will be taking over the pond. When you then

have to clear out the pond it will be a muddy, messy business, and the roots will be a tangled mass. Containers enable you to control growth, keep the more vigorous types under control, and make the job of cleaning out the pond or re-planting very much easier.

Oxygenating plants are often sold in bunches of cuttings, held together with a strip of lead. If you just drop these into the water the stems will probably rot where they have been crushed by the weight and bits of plant will simply float about. Bury the bottom of the shoots (with the lead strip) in compost or gravel, then the cuttings will soon root and anchor themselves.

SUITABLE AQUATIC PLANTS

The list of aquatic plants below includes most of those that you are likely to encounter in garden centres and specialist nurseries. Space limitations restrict descriptions, but just as important as what a plant looks like is how it grows and performs as a good pond plant. To help you distinguish those which are most likely to please from those that may disappoint, a star rating has been given to each entry. Three specialist aquatic plant growers were asked to rate each one according to the descriptions given below. The ratings for each plant are based on their combined experience.

Key to ratings Beside each plant you will find a rating of between one and five stars. These indicate what you might expect from the plant in terms of display, ease of cultivation, or rate of growth. Unless you want a plant for a particular purpose, the higher the number of stars the more likely you are to find it a desirable plant. Of course, some of the plants with fewer stars may also make very good pond plants, and they will add variety and interest once you have established a basic collection of the more popular plants. Waterlilies are dealt with separately on page pp. 86 – 8).

*****Very decorative and easy. Worth including in a starter collection.
****Very decorative, but may be slow to mature, or be more difficult to grow easily or well; or may be too large for a small pool.
***Useful and decorative.
**Useful and decorative, but may be slow to establish well enough for an impressive display; or you may have to provide winter protection.
*Worth growing if you already have the more desirable and important plants.
+Introduce only after careful consideration. Rampant and may become a nuisance and difficult to control.

Planting depth (PD) is the depth of water above the soil or compost.

DEEP-WATER AQUATICS

The plants below, together with the nymphaeas (waterlilies), which will be found on page pp. 86 – 8), are usually described as deep-water aquatics. Do not let this mislead you into thinking that they must necessarily have *deep* water; most will be happy covered with as little as 15 cm (6 in) of water. It is better to regard them as plants for the centre of the pool rather than the marginal shelf.

Aponogeton distachyus (water hawthorn)*** The curious white, forked flowers have conspicuous black anthers. This plant flowers freely in early summer and sporadically into late autumn and is fragrant. The dull green, almost oblong, strap-like floating leaves are present almost all year. PD: 15 – 45 cm (6 – 18 in).
Nuphar lutea (yellow pondlily, brandy bottle) + The bottle-shaped

Aponogeton distachyus, the water hawthorn, one of the most useful deep-water aquatic plants, coming into flower in spring and continuing into autumn.

Orontium aquaticum, the golden club, a strange-looking plant that often attracts comment.

yellow flowers, about 5 cm (2 in) across, have a sickly odour. There are masses of leathery, dark green floating leaves. It is best grown in deep water in spots unsuitable for the nymphaeas (waterlilies). PD: 0.3–1.5m (1–5 ft).

Orontium aquaticum (golden club)**** The poker-like flowers, with bright yellow tips, are carried well clear of the water, in mid and late spring. PD: 8–45 cm (3–18 in).

Nymphaea See waterlilies (page 86).

Nymphoides peltata (Villarsia nymphoides) (water fringe)* Like a miniature yellow waterlily, the flowers, held clear of the water, appear in late summer. The floating leaves, about 8 cm (3 in) across, are mottled brown. The plant sold as *Villarsia bennetii* is similar. PD: 10–30 cm (4–12 in).

Villarsia See Nymphoides.

Waterlilies See page 86.

MARGINAL PLANTS

'Marginal' plants can be grown in shallow water or in soil that is permanently damp. *The planting depth is measured from soil level, not the base of the pond.* A plant that grows best in 10 cm (4 in) of water may be suitable for a 25 cm (10 in) shelf if it is planted in a 15 cm (6 in) deep pot or basket.

Acorus calamus (sweet flag, sweet- scented rush)★ This rush has flat, linear leaves, like an iris, and greenish-yellow or brownish horn-like flowers. The variety 'Variegatus'★★★★★ is a more attractive plant, having 75 cm (2½ ft) leaves striped green and cream. PD: 8–13 cm (3–5 in).

A. gramineus 'Variegatus'★★★★★ This plant has slender, almost grass-like leaves with a white stripe. About 30 cm (1 ft) high. PD: 8–13 cm (3–5 in).

Alisma parviflora★★ Pyramidal panicles of small white flowers are produced. Height 45 cm (1½ ft). PD: 8–13 cm (3–5 in).

A. plantago (water plantain)★ This species has small pink and white flowers and broad, lance-shaped, long-stalked leaves. Height 60 cm (2 ft). PD: 0–15 cm (0–6 in).

Acorus gramineus 'Variegata', useful for the water's edge.

Butomus umbellatus, the flowering rush. The flower heads are attractive, but the plant lacks impact from a distance.

Caltha palustris 'Flore Pleno', the double marsh marigold.

Caltha polypetala, a large, bold plant that is best for a large pool.

Butomus umbellatus (flowering rush)★★★ The clusters of small, red-centred flowers on tall stems are produced in late summer and early autumn. The leaves are rush-like. Height 75 cm (2½ ft). PD: 8 – 13 cm (3 – 5 in).

Calla palustris (bog arum)★★★★ This has small white spathes like small arum lilies, and glossy, heart-shaped leaves. It has a spreading habit. Height 15 cm (6 in). PD: 5 – 10 cm (2 – 4 in).

Caltha palustris (marsh marigold, kingcup)★★★ There are large, buttercup-like bright yellow flowers. 'Flore Pleno' or 'Plena' (★★★★) is double, producing yellow pompons. 'Alba' (★★★) is white. Height 15 – 30 cm (6 – 12 in). PD: 0 – 5 cm (0 – 2 in).

C. polypetala (giant marsh marigold)★★ The single yellow flowers are sometimes about 8 cm (3 in) across in spring. Height 60 – 90 cm (2 – 3 ft). PD: 8 – 13 cm (3 – 5 in).

Cotula coronopifolia (brass buttons)★★★ Small yellow, button-like flowers are produced throughout the summer. The leaves are aromatic when crushed. Height 23 cm (9 in). PD: 0 – 13 cm (0 – 5 in).

Cyperus longus (ornamental rush,

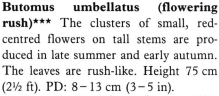

A variegated cyperus in a greenhouse pool – this one is not hardy.

Cyperus, an umbrella grass related to the one used as a houseplant.

Glyceria aquatica, a variegated water grass.

sweet galingale) + The grass-like stems have leaves radiating umbrella-like at the top. Height 90 cm (3 ft). It will not stand severe frosts. *C. alternifolius* (★★) is similar but smaller and not frost-hardy. *C. vegatus (C. eragrostis)* (★) grows to about 60 cm (2 ft) and is hardy. PD: 5 – 15 cm (2 – 6 in).
Eriophorum angustifolium (cotton grass)★ This plant has sedge-like stems, and silky white cotton-like tufts. Height 30 cm (1 ft). *E. latifolium* (★) has broader, flatter leaves, and is slightly taller. PD: 0 – 13 cm (0 – 5 in).
Glyceria maxima 'Variegata' (G.

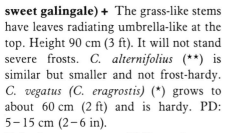

73

Irises in a rectangular plastic planter. Covering the surface with gravel looks better and prevents fish stirring up the compost.

spectabilis 'Variegata', G. aquatica 'Variegata') (variegated water grass)*** This grass has leaves striped yellow and white. Height 60 cm (2 ft). It can become invasive. PD: 5 – 13 cm (2 – 5 in).

Houttuynia cordata** This plant has blue-green heart-shaped leaves, reddish stems, and cone-shaped spikes of white, four petalled flowers in late summer. 'Plena' (***) has double flowers. Height 15 – 30 cm (6 – 12 in). PD: 5 – 10 cm (2 – 4 in).

Iris laevigata***** This species has typical iris leaves, and blue flowers in

Menyanthes trifoliata, the bog bean, a plant for shallow water. It has white fringed flowers in late spring.

A *Mimulus luteus* hybrid – easy to grow and easy to raise from seed or cuttings.

early summer, and often again in autumn. Height 60–75 cm (2–2½ ft). There are many varieties including 'Atropurpurea' (*****), 'Colchesteri' (*****), 'Mottled Beauty' (*****), 'Rose Queen' (***), and 'Snowdrift' (*****). 'Variegata' (*****) is especially attractive because of the cream-striped foliage. PD: 5–10 cm (2–4 in).

I. pseudacorus (yellow flag) + Yellow flag has sword-like leaves and bold yellow flowers on 60–90 cm (2–3 ft) stems. Varieties include 'Golden Queen' (+) and 'Sulphur Queen' (*). 'Variegata' (*) has yellow leaf variegation, but this fades with the advancing season. PD: 5–13 cm (2–5 in).

I. versicolor***** The violet-blue flowers are veined purple and splashed gold. 'Kermesina' (*****) is claret with similar markings. Height: 45 cm (1½ ft). PD: 5–10 cm (2–4 in).

Juncus effusus 'Spiralis' (corkscrew rush)** The rush-like leaves are twisted like a corkscrew. Height about 60 cm (2 ft). PD: 8–13 cm (3–5 in).

Mentha aquatica (water mint)*** This plant has aromatic leaves, lilac flowers, and a spreading habit. Height: 23–30 cm (9–12 in). PD: 0–8 cm (0–3 in).

Menyanthes trifoliata (bog bean)** The short spikes of white flowers tinged pink are produced in late spring and early summer. The leaves resemble those of broad beans. Height 23 cm (9 in). PD: 5–10 cm (2–4 in).

Mimulus luteus (monkey flower, yellow money musk)* The plant sold as *M. luteus* is sometimes the species *M. guttatus*. The yellow flowers blotched red are present all summer. There are many hybrids, which have a wider colour range. It seeds itself freely. Height 30 cm (1 ft). PD: 0–5 cm (0–2 in).

M. ringens (lavender musk)** This species has lavender-blue flowers. Height 45 cm (1½ ft). PD: 8–13 cm (3–5 in).

Myosotis palustris (M. scorpioides) (water forget-me-not)* Deep blue forget-me-not flowers are produced in early summer. Height 15 cm (6 in). PD: 0–8 cm (0–3 in).

Myriophyllum proserpinacoides (M. brasiliense, M. aquaticum) (milfoil, parrot's feather)** The feathery light green leaves rise about 15–20 cm (6–8 in) out of the water. The exposed parts turn crimson in autumn; the rest stays green. PD: 8–15 cm (3–6 in).

Peltandra virginica (arrow arum)** This plant has glossy, arrow-shaped leaves, and arum-like green flowers in

Myriophyllum proserpinacoides, a water milfoil.

mid-spring. Height 60 cm (2 ft). PD: 8 – 15 cm (3 – 6 in).

Pontederia cordata (pickerel weed)***** Bold, glossy leaves are held on 60 cm (2 ft) stems, and there are spikes of blue flowers in late summer. PD: 8 – 13 cm (3 – 5 in).

Ranunculus flammula (lesser spearwort)** Buttercup-like flowers are produced on wiry stems, over dark green leaves. Height 30 cm (1 ft). PD: 0 – 8 cm (0 – 3 in).

R. lingua 'Grandiflora' (greater spearwort) + There are narrow, dark green leaves and yellow flowers for much of the summer. Height 60 cm (2 ft). PD: 0 – 8 cm (0 – 3 in).

Sagittaria japonica (arrowhead)**** The white flowers have yellow centres, and there are broad, three-pointed leaves. Height 75 cm (2½ ft). 'Plena' or 'Flore Pleno' (*****) has double white flowers, but is a shorter plant. PD: 8 – 13 cm (3 – 5 in).

A well-established clump of *Pontederia cordata*.

Ranunculus lingua 'Grandiflora' has buttercup-like flowers over a long period.

S. sagittifolia (swamp potato, arrowhead)* The leaves that emerge are arrow-shaped, and the flowers are white. Height 30 – 45 cm (1 – 1½ ft). PD: 8 – 13 cm (3 – 5 in).

Saururus cernuus (swamp lily, lizard's tail)**** This plant has heart-shaped leaves and nodding sprays of creamy-white flowers in mid- and late summer. Height 60 cm (2 ft). PD: 0 – 5 cm (0 – 2 in).

Scirpus albescens (bulrush)**** The rushy stems are about 1.2 m (4 ft) high, striped green and white. Height 90 cm (3 ft). PD: 8 – 13 cm (3 – 5 in).

S. tabernaemontani 'Zebrinus' (often listed as *S. zebrinus*) (zebra rush)***** The quill-like leaves are banded green and white. Height about 90 cm (3 ft). PD: 8 – 15 cm (3 – 5 in).

Sparganium ramosum (bur reed) + This is a coarse, rush-like plant with linear leaves, and heads of brownish-

Sagittaria sagittifolia, the common arrowhead.

Scirpus tabernaemonti 'Zebrinus', an unusual plant with horizontally-striped leaves.

green flowers. The roots are liable to damage a pool liner. It can be rampant. Height 60–90 cm (2–3 ft). PD: 8–13 cm (3–5 in).

Typha angustifolia (reedmace) + This plant has the large, flat leaves and poker-like flower heads that many people wrongly call bulrushes. The spikes reach 1.8 m (6 ft). It is very rampant. PD: 0–15 cm (0–6 in).

T. latifolia (great reedmace, common catstail) + This is a larger version growing up to 2.4 m (8 ft). It is rampant. PD: 8–13 cm (3–5 in).

T. minima**** This is a dwarf, non-rampant reedmace, growing to about 45 cm (1½ ft). PD: 0–10 cm (0–4 in).

T. laxmannii (T. stenophylla) (small reedmace) + One of the more

restrained reedmaces, this species grows to about 90 cm (3 ft). PD: 0–15 cm (0–6 in).

Veronica beccabunga (brooklime)* The bright blue flowers are carried in the leaf axils, all summer. Height 23 cm (9 in). PD: 0–10 cm (0–4 in).

SUBMERGED AQUATICS

***Visually attractive submerged aquatic. Well worth introducing.
**Not attractive, but very useful for its oxygenating role.
*Not of such merit as previous two groups.

*Callitriche palustris (C. verna)****
Ceratophyllum demersum (hornwort)***

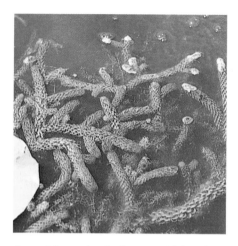

Lagarosiphon major, also known as *Elodea crispa*, a popular oxygenating plant.

Tillaea recurva, one of the best oxygenating plants, useful for controlling green water.

*Egeria densa (Elodea densa)**
Eleocharis acicularis (hair grass)**
Elodea canadensis (Canadian pondweed)**
Fontinalis antipyretica (willow moss)**
Hottonia palustris (water violet)***
*Lagarosiphon major (Elodea crispa)**
Myriophyllum spicatum (milfoil)***
M. verticillatum (milfoil)***
Potamogeton crispus (curled pondweed)**
Ranunculus aquatilis (water crowfoot)**
*Tillaea recurva****

FLOATING PLANTS

***Showy.
**Not especially showy, but interesting.
*Invasive and best avoided.
Azolla caroliniana (fairy moss)***
Hydrocharis morsus-ranae (frogbit)**
Lemna minor (common duckweed)*
L. gibba (thick duckweed)*
L. polyrrhiza (greater duckweed)*
L. trisulca (ivy-leaved duckweed)**
Stratiotes aloides (water soldier)***
Trapa natans (water chestnut)**

Tender floating plants There are two very attractive tender floating plants that you may find offered. The water hyacinth *(Eichhornia crassipes)* has beautiful flowers, given the right conditions. Outdoors the plant will multiply and spread rapidly, but flowers will be very elusive. The water lettuce *(Pistia stratiotes)* is a beautiful plant but more suited for the aquarium than the pond. Both these must be overwintered in a frost-free tank indoors.

Azolla caroliniana, a plant that will soon form a carpet over the surface, yet is not difficult to control. Its colour is affected by temperature – in this picture the green plants on the left have been grown in warm water, the reddish plants on the right in cold water. In the pond they usually turn reddish with the approach of autumn.

One of the lemnas or duckweeds. As a rule these should be avoided as they multiply rapidly and are very difficult to eliminate.

Stratiotes aloides, a rosette-forming plant that floats just beneath the water for most of the summer, coming to the surface to bloom. It sinks to the bottom in autumn.

Trapa natans, the water chestnut. The horned fruit is visible on the gravel.

Astilbes will grow perfectly well in a herbaceous border, but they look at their best close to water.

BOG PLANTS

These plants are all suitable for bog or waterside planting. Those of special merit are followed by a star (*).

Antholyza paniculata 'Major'
Astilbe hybrids*
Bergenia cordifolia
Crocosmia 'Lucifer'
*Gunnera manicata**
Helxine soleirolii (Soleirolia soleirolii)
Hemerocallis hybrids*
Hosta spp.*

Gunnera manicata, surely one of the most imposing waterside plants, but with mature leaves 1.5 m (5 ft) or more across it is only for a large pool.

Iris bulleyana
I. chrysographes
I. cristata
I. dykesii
I. foetidissima
I. forestii
I. kaempferi (and varieties)*
I. longipetala
I. pallida 'Variegata'*
I. sibirica (and varieties)
Ligularia clivorum 'Desdemona'
L. stenocephala 'The Rocket'
Lobelia cardinalis or *L. fulgens**
*L. vedrariensis**
*Lysichitum americanum**
*L. camtschatcense**
Mimulus cardinalis
M. bartonius
Miscanthus sacchariflorus

Iris kaempferi, sometimes called the Japanese clematis-flowered iris. A beautiful bog plant.

M. sinensis 'Gracillimus'
Osmunda regalis
Peltiphyllum peltatum★
Phalaris arundinaecea 'Picta'
Phalaris picta
Primula apicola
P. beesiana
P. bulleyana
P. chungensis
P. denticulata
P. farinosa
P. florindae★
P. helodoxa
P. involucrata
P. japonica (and varieties)

P. pulverulenta
P. rosea
P. secundiflora
P. sieboldii
P. sikkimensis
P. vialii
Rheum palmatum 'Rubrum'★
Rogersia aesculifolia
R. pinnata (and hybrids)
Schizostylis coccinea★
Spartina pectinata
Stipa gigantea
Trollius europaeus
Trollius hybrids★

Osmunda regalis, a large and imposing fern for the waterside. The fronds turn an attractive yellow in autumn.

There are so many waterlilies, the vast majority of them excellent plants, that it has been necessary to whittle them down to 24 for inclusion in this book; not only for reasons of space, but also to make selection easier. A very long list of good plants is often confusing because you are still left wondering which of them you should try. To make selection easier, in the table below they are arranged by colour, with vigour and planting depth given so that you can choose one from that colour range for the depth and size of your pond.

Nymphaea 'Escarboucle', one of the best waterlilies for a medium-sized or large pool, is also known as 'Aflame'.

A few of these waterlilies are true species (*Nymphaea candida* for instance) and some are varieties of species (such as *N. pygmaea* 'Helvola'), but in catalogues and on plant labels you are likely to find all the names presented as varieties, and that approach has been adopted here.

In the 'Vigour' column, the following abbreviations have been used.

M = miniature, suitable for sinks and tubs.

S = small.

I = intermediate.

V = vigorous, for large pools or lakes.

'Planting depth' is the depth of water above the soil. Opinions regarding ideal planting depths vary considerably, and most of the waterlilies in this table will grow perfectly well in water a few inches shallower, and in many cases even a foot (30 cm) deeper, than indicated. Use the planting depths as an approximate guide.

Nymphaea 'Froebeli', a free-flowering variety ideal for a small pond or a barrel pool.

Nymphaea 'James Brydon', a variety raised in the United States.

Nymphaea × *marliacea* 'Chromatella' dates from 1877. It is also known as 'Golden Cup'.

Nymphaea 'Masaniello', a variety introduced in 1908 but still popular.

Nymphaea pygmaea 'Helvola' is a miniature waterlily and a real gem for a shallow container.

Nymphaea 'Rose Arey', one of the best rose-pink waterlilies.

Variety	Vigour	Planting depth
RED VARIETIES		
Conqueror	I–V	30–75 cm (12–30 in)
Escarboucle	I–V	30–75 cm (12–30 in)
Froebeli	S	15–45 cm (6–18 in)
James Brydon	S–I	30–60 cm (12–24 in)
Laydekeri Purpurata	M	15–45 cm (6–18 in)
Rene Gerard	I	23–60 cm (9–24 in)
William Falconer	I	23–45 cm (9–18 in)
YELLOW VARIETIES		
Colonel A.J. Welch	V	30–90 cm (12–36 in)
Marliacea Chromatella	I	30–75 cm (12–30 in)
Pygmaea Helvola	M	10–23 cm (4–9 in)
PINK VARIETIES		
Amabilis	I–V	30–60 cm (12–24 in)
Laydekeri Lilacea	M–S	10–30 cm (4–12 in)
Marliacea Rosea	I–V	30–75 cm (12–30 in)
Masaniello	I–V	23–90 cm (9–36 in)
Mme Wilfron Gonnêre	I	23–45 cm (9–18 in)
Mrs Richmond	I–V	23–75 cm (9–30 in)
Rose Arey	S–I	23–45 cm (9–18 in)
WHITE VARIETIES		
Albatross	I	15–45 cm (6–18 in)
Candida	M	10–23 cm (4–9 in)
Gladstoniana	V	45–90 cm (18–36 in)
Gonnêre	I	23–60 cm (9–24 in)
Odorata Alba	I	23–45 cm (9–18 in)
Pygmaea Alba	M	10–23 cm (4–9 in)
OTHER COLOURS		
Paul Hariot (opens pale yellow, deepens to copper-red)	S	15–30 cm (6–12 in)

7·THE FISH

Fish will add another dimension to your water garden. The plants may be beautiful but fish provide an element of suspense and surprise. You never know where they are going to be, even whether you will see some types at all some days. When they start breeding there is the excitement of watching the fry grow, wondering what kind they are and perhaps what colour or markings they will have. Fish are dynamic inhabitants of the pond, and can become real pets.

As with most aspects of water gardening, there are some snags and drawbacks as well as enormous rewards. If you approach fish-keeping realistically, however, the problems will be few and the delights many.

Fish will help to make the pond lively, colourful and interesting. They also have a practical use: they will help to control mosquitoes, gnats and midges by eating them (or at least those stages of the life cycle that take place in or near water). They will also eat the larval or egg stages of many pests of water plants, such as aphids and waterlily beetles.

CHOOSING FISH

In comparison with tropical fish-keeping,
the range of cold-water fish available is relatively small, but none the less interesting for that. It should also make the choice of suitable fish relatively easy.

Bronze carp   This is the name used by aquarists to describe any bronze-coloured carp-like fish, but usually uncoloured goldfish are meant. Although one would not want to condemn them, they cannot really be recommended because they will breed with your coloured goldfish and the bronze colour will predominate in their progeny.

Common carp *(Cyprinus carpio)* Strictly a fish for a large pond. It has a chubby body, narrow tapering head and four hanging barbels. The colouring is dull, usually silvery or bronze. Although a playful fish, it has a habit of stirring up mud while routing for insects.

There are more interesting variations, such as the Chinese red carp or Higoi, a salmon or orange-pink fish, or the bronze mirror carp with one or two rows of greatly enlarged, mirror-like scales. These fish can look attractive in a large aquarium, but will be far more difficult to see in the dirtier water of a pond.

Catfish   This rather vague title is

Koi carp and goldfish are among the most attractive pond fish, and unlike some fish are usually easy to see.

commonly given to several species of fish, such as the horned pout *(Ameiurus nebulosus)*, brown bullhead *(Ictalyrus nebulosus)*, and the German wels or waller *(Silurus glanis)*. They all have long, whisker-like barbels and are rather ugly-looking.

They are scavengers, eating food missed or rejected by the other fish found on the floor of the pond. Their taste extends to insects and worms, and even the tails of fancy goldfish, and the fry of any. They are so pugnacious that slower-moving more docile fish may be harried unmercifully.

Although traditionally thought of as 'good' for the pond, they are unnecessary, and on balance probably do more harm than good. You certainly will not see much of them.

Crucian carp *(Carassius carassius)* Rather like a deep-bodied, chocolate or bronze-coloured common carp, but lacking its pendent barbels and depressed head. Unfortunately it does not show up well in a pond.

Goldfish *(Carassius auratus auratus)* It is a pity that goldfish are so common. They must surely be one of the best-known fish, and for that reason are sometimes frowned upon as being too common. They are undoubtedly among the finest pond fish. Not only are they friendly fish easily tamed, but they show up well and are among the most visible fish in a pond.

If the common gold goldfish does not appeal, then there are many varieties that are different in shape or colour. Colours range from red, pink and gold, through orange to yellow and pearl and even black. Then there are the forms with modified tails and even modified eyes; some beautiful, some grotesque. Some of these are illustrated below.

Shubunkins are an unusual form of goldfish; it is sometimes hard to realise that they are not a distinct species. They have mainly transparent scales, and are usually spotted or blotched in shades of blue, red, orange, and white. There are fantail forms. Shubunkins are sometimes called calico fish.

The more exotic forms of goldfish are less hardy than the common kind, and they will benefit from some protection, possibly indoors, in winter, or at least a water depth of 45 cm (18 in) so that they can take refuge during very severe weather.

Green tench *(Tinca tinca)* A scavenging fish, the green tench will spend most of its time on the bottom, so you will hardly ever see it. There is also a golden form that looks good in an aquarium but is hardly more visible than the green variety in a pond. The green tench has a short and rather broad olive-green body, narrow, tapering head, and rather square tail.

Gudgeon *(Gobio gobio)* Gudgeons are not pretty fish. They have elongated, rather cylindrical greyish-brown bodies, tails and large heads with quite prominent eyes and short barbels hanging down from the mouth. They are well known to anglers. As they spend much of their time routing around on the bottom, and are not colourful or large fish, they will add little interest to the

Releasing a golden orfe into the water after a period of time in the bag floating on the water to balance the temperature.

pond, although they can be tamed if fed regularly.

Koi carp Most of the carp family are useful in ponds, the goldfish especially, but none of them can match the Koi carp. These beauties are big, fast-growing, usually wonderfully marked and coloured, and easily tamed. There is just one drawback: they need a large pond and are unsuitable for anything less than say 4.5m² (50 sq ft) surface area. They also like a depth of at least 1 m (3 ft).

Colours include red, gold, orange, yellow, pink, bronze, blue-grey, silver, and white. Sometimes they are all one colour; others are beautifully marked or blotched with other colours.

Koi carp tend to rummage on the bottom and may stir up a lot of mud. For this reason, and because they need well-aerated water, a filter system will certainly help (see page 108).

If you dismiss goldfish as common you will miss some of the pond's brightest inhabitants.

They may grow large, and if not limited by the size of the pool often grow 60 cm (2 ft) long and may attain 2 kg (4½ lb) in weight. Large fish are expensive to buy (outstanding specimens will be *very* expensive) but as they grow so quickly you will not be disappointed if you start with young, inexpensive specimens.

The fish that you buy from garden centres will probably be labelled Koi carp, but specialist suppliers may offer named forms (for instance 'Shiro-ogen' is a pure white form).

Minnow *(Phoxinus phoxinus)* Minnows are small fish that rarely exceed 10 cm (4 in), but they can help to enliven a pool by their active, darting movements, seen as flashes of silvery-grey. They have green-brown backs and silvery-grey sides with darker bands. The males turn very dark, almost black, during the breeding season with a reddish belly.

To see minnows at their best they need to be in a shoal, so introduce a worthwhile number, not just one or two.

Orfe *(Idus idus)* These are beautiful fish, especially in the golden form (the ordinary species is silvery). Young fish especially look rather like young carrots swimming about. They are sleeker than goldfish (and have a black mark on the head, which is lost as the fish mature) and are altogether more active. They may reach 30 cm (1 ft) or more, but seldom breed in Britain.

They feed and swim near the surface, so you should see a lot of them, but they are shoaling fish and need plenty of companions to be seen at their best.

There are two drawbacks. One is that they need a large pond to be successful (and even then they are unlikely to breed). The other is that being active fish they become very vulnerable if the carbon dioxide level builds up, which is especially likely in hot weather in the summer. Unless the water is well aerated with either a waterfall or fountain, you may suddenly find most of them dead within a very short period in very hot summer weather.

Roach *(Rutilus rutilus)* Well known to fishermen, this fish is silvery, with bright red irises to the eyes. It will adapt easily to pond life but is not very useful because its combination of colouring and midwater habit mean you will not see much of it.

Rudd *(Scardinius erythrophthalmus)* The common rudd is not usually offered for sale, but the silver and golden forms may sometimes be found where fish are sold. The silvery one is, as its name implies, silvery in appearance, with reddish fins; the golden one has a golden metallic lustre. Rudd are sleek fish, swimming with rapid darting, almost nervous movements. They are useful if you want to add a little more interest to the pond, but do not expect them to be visible or especially interesting fish.

Shubunkin – see goldfish.

Stickleback *(Gasterosteus* spp*)* Not fish to be introduced into the pond. Although only small (up to 5 cm/2 in or so), they are pugnacious fish that will regard more docile species as fair game.

BUYING FISH

Many of the fish offered for sale will have been imported. They may not have been acclimatised very well, and they may be under stress and possibly under-nourished. For that reason it is always worth looking at the fish carefully before you buy them, and isolating them in a quarantine pool in case diseases or pests manifest themselves. Fish, like humans, are more vulnerable to illness if under stress.

Healthy fish will be active and alert, and swim with erect fins. Avoid fish with drooping fins, and any with a whitish film over their eyes. Eyes should be bright.

Many fish (Koi carp are an exception) tend to lose their bright colouring if they have been in the supplier's tanks for a few weeks. This is no bad thing, because you know the fish have had a chance to become acclimatised and they will soon regain their brighter colouring once they are in a pond again. Examine their bodies and fins carefully, and be reluctant to accept any with lost scales (though the larger the fish the more likely you are to have to accept this kind of damage). Do not buy any with ulcers or white spots. In fact, if you find any with small white spots, it is best to avoid all fish in the same tank.

Some carp suffer from a disease that gives them a large head, so avoid any that seem to have a larger than normal head and a narrow or pinched body.

A few fish develop characteristic colouring or habits if they are about to die. Green tench and catfish become very dark, almost black. The dumpy fantail goldfish often suffer from swimbladder disorders, so avoid any that swim upside-down or in an erratic manner.

FISH BY POST

You can buy fish by mail order. It is not advisable if you have the option of collecting your fish, for then you can choose the individual ones that you want, and you know what you are buying. The fish are also likely to suffer less stress. Sometimes, however, because of where you live, or because you want a fish that you are unable to buy locally, you may have to send away for them.

FISH FROM THE WILD

Some of the fish described in this chapter may be native fish. You may need permission to take the fish away if you catch them, but even so introducing wild fish is not really a good idea: they may be carrying diseases to which they have become resistant but which could be disastrous to the established pond fish.

Bubble-eye Goldfish

Celestial Goldfish

Sarasa Comet

Fantail Goldfish

Lionhead Goldfish

Blue Comet or Shubunkin

Koi Carp

Common Goldfish

Golden Orfe

Mirror Carp

Tench

95

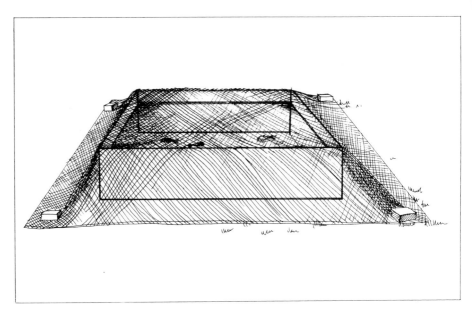

You can go some way to overcoming this problem by putting them in quarantine and treating them routinely with suitable medicaments.

The quarantine pond A quarantine pool can be made from some modest container if the fish are not large; a child's inflatable paddling pool is a useful quarantine pond as it can be folded up and put away when not needed. If you use a shallow container as a quarantine pool, cover the top with fine-mesh netting (such as fruit netting) to prevent the fish jumping out. You can weight the net down at the edges with bricks. Fill the quarantine pool several days before the fish arrive, to give the chlorine a chance to dissipate.

You may prefer to leave the new fish

An improvised pond is useful when cleaning out the proper pond or to isolate new or ailing fish. A child's folding paddling pool is perfectly adequate, but cover it with a net to keep the fish in and the cats out.

for a couple of weeks to see whether any symptoms appear, or you can give them some routine treatments anyway as a precaution. You could use a preparation for treating any flukes, anchor worms or fish lice that might be present, then 10 days later use an anti-bacterial treatment. Then wait another week to see if any specific problems arise.

RELEASING THE FISH

Fish are sensitive to rapid changes in water temperature, so try to avoid releasing the fish straight into the pond as soon as you get home. Whether you buy your fish from a garden centre, pet shop, or by mail order, they will almost certainly arrive in a polythene bag that contains plenty of air space. If you are buying by post, or if you go to a specialist supplier and he knows that you have a long way to travel, oxygen will be used to inflate the bag.

To give the water in the bag a chance to adjust slowly to the temperature of the pond, float the bag on the pond or quarantine tank for about half an hour. If the weather is very hot, keep the bag floating in a shady area, otherwise the rapid build-up of heat in the bag may do more harm than releasing them immediately.

NUMBERS OF FISH

One should not be dogmatic about how many fish a particular pond will support. It depends on many things: the number of oxygenating plants it contains, whether you are going to give them supplementary feeding, and whether you have installed a filtration system. There are however, some useful guidelines.

Work on the basis of 2 in of fish for every 1 sq ft of surface (5 cm for each 0.1 m^2). So a pond 8×4 ft (32 sq ft) would support about (64 in) of fish. Put another way, 32 fish 2 in long, or about 11 fish 6 in long, and so on. A deeper pond will not really support more fish than a shallower one with the same surface area, as it is the surface that is the pond's 'lung'.

It is better to understock rather than overstock, especially as fish grow (not to mention breed) and this will upset your initial calculations. It is best to allow for growth, and on the basis of an average fish being 4 in (10 cm) long after a few years (make a separate calculation for large fish such as Koi carp) not to exceed one fish to 2 sq ft (0.2m^2). So our theoretical pond of 32 sq ft should not contain more than 16 fish.

FEEDING FISH

In large stretches of water, fish manage with what nature provides. In a small garden pool, supplementary feeding is necessary, though overfeeding must be guarded against. Feeding is unwise between late autumn and early spring when the fish are less active. For the rest of the year you can feed say three times a week; but give them only as much as they can eat in five minutes. In summer you might want to feed daily to tame the fish. If you always feed from the same place many fish will become used to you as the supplier of food and will take titbits from your hand.

You can feed them things like chopped worms, chopped egg, and minced meat, but proprietary balanced fish foods are both convenient and adequate. Floating pellets and flakes have the advantage of giving you a better view of the fish feeding, and pellets are less likely than

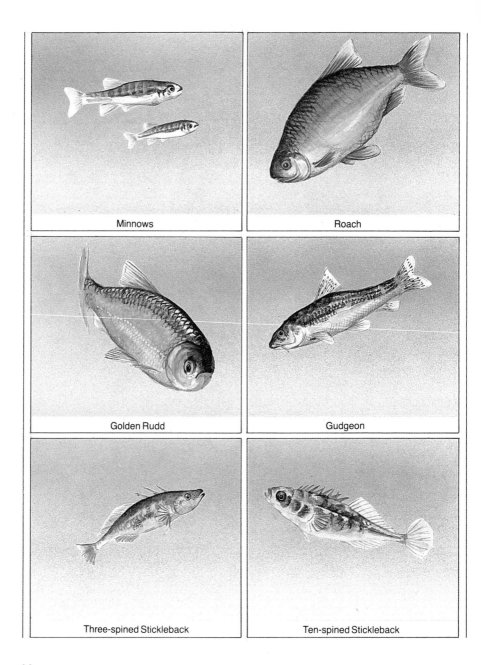

Minnows

Roach

Golden Rudd

Gudgeon

Three-spined Stickleback

Ten-spined Stickleback

flakes to blow out of reach of the fish on a windy day.

Daphnia can be cultured to provide a source of much-appreciated food in the summer. Use a tub of water with about 2.5 cm (1 in) of soil in the base, then once the soil has settled introduce a jar of live daphnia. They will multiply rapidly, and you can remove some each week to feed to your pond fish, topping up the tub with the same amount of water.

BREEDING

Whether you like it or not, your fish are almost certainly going to breed. It is great fun discovering the tiny, almost transparent fry if you have not previously noticed the eggs, and watching them develop.

You may be alarmed at the sheer number of fry at first, and wonder how you are going to dispose of them all. If you do nothing, the numbers will steadily decrease as they get eaten by the larger fish. If you want to raise as many fish as possible, the eggs will have to be removed into another pond, or failing this the fry netted and transferred.

Fish prefer to spawn among plants in shallow water, and if you provide seed trays on the marginal shelf thickly planted with oxygenators they will probably spawn among these. If you see fish chasing each other, sometimes almost pushing each other out of the water, any time between mid-spring and late summer, they are probably spawning. They are stimulated by both warmth and light intensity.

The eggs normally hatch in about five days if the temperature is about 21°C (70°F), but they will take longer in cooler weather. Once the fry have eaten their yolk sacs, they feed on tiny organisms that they find in the water, but you can buy special fry food that will encourage rapid growth.

Once the fry are large enough to be recognisable you may be disappointed by their colouring. Goldfish in particular can be disconcerting if you have never seen young goldfish. The colour is a drab olive, although this will usually change gradually to gold during the next couple of years. Some, however, remain dark. If you have any intention of breeding, all these darker or less desirable forms should be discarded – but wait until you are sure the colour is not going to change. You can make this decision after 18 months or when the fish are 7.5 cm (3 in) long.

8·THE NATURALIST'S POOL

With absolutely no effort on your part, the pond will gradually (but quite rapidly) become colonised by creatures of all kinds: from microscopic pond organisms to large amphibians such as frogs and newts. When you come to clean out your pond, or lift a plant for any reason, you will probably be confronted with all kinds of weird creatures, some such as the dragonfly nymphs so grotesque and almost frightening that it is hard to imagine they could turn into the attractive above-surface forms with which we are more familiar.

Some of the uninvited visitors will do no harm and may even be beneficial; others are decidedly unwelcome. In this brief chapter it is impossible to open up the fascinating underwater world that waits for anyone willing to look; it can only highlight some of the 'goodies' and the 'baddies' that you may wonder about.

AMPHIBIANS

Amphibians possess lungs and may live on land for much of their time, but they return to water to breed, usually in spring or early summer. Generally they stay in the vicinity of the pond for the rest of the year. Like fish, they are cold-blooded and temperature affects their body and its activities. In winter they become torpid and sluggish, and may hibernate until spring.

Frogs are the amphibians most associated with ponds, and, as they eat slugs and many other enemies of the gardener, should be encouraged. They will usually be there, lurking beneath or behind stones or snuggling among the waterside vegetation; it is at the mating season that you cannot help but notice them. They can make quite a noise in the evening when possibly dozens of them are giving mating calls. You might even hear them while you are indoors. If you go out with a torch the chances are you will find some of the males clasping their mates beneath them, gripping behind their front legs. By morning you can expect to find the masses of spawn among submerged aquatics such as elodeas.

The only harm that frogs may occasionally do is caused by solitary males clasping a fish in desperation for a mate, but the chance of this happening and doing any lasting harm is remote.

The common British frog is *Rana temporaria*, which grows to about 10 cm (4 in) long, though there are some less common species that have become

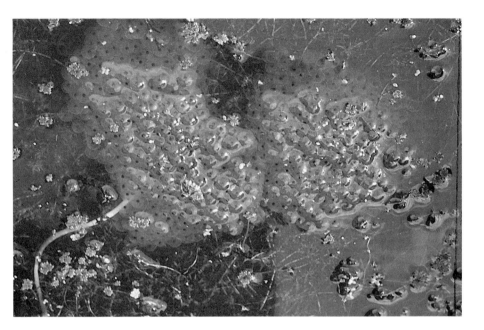

Frog spawn is usually laid in densely matted water plants such as elodea.

established in some areas, and of course in places like the United States a number of different species are encountered.

Toads are often confused with frogs, but for some reason always seem less welcome. They differ from frogs in having shorter legs, which means that they crawl rather than hop, and instead of being smooth the skin is warty in appearance. In Britain, the one you are likely to see is *Bufo bufo*, the common toad, which reaches about 15 cm (6 in) long. It usually only visits the pond for breeding. The spawn is laid in long chains rather than in a mass.

The easiest way to introduce frogs or toads to the pond is as spawn, though most of the tadpoles are likely to be eaten by fish.

Newts The most widespread newt in Britain is the common newt, *Triturus vulgaris*. It is about 10 cm (4 in) long. The male has an orange-red belly and black blotches over its body, and in spring develops a smooth ridge down its back. The female is brownish, and less spectacular. Like frogs the eggs hatch into tadpoles and gradually change into the form that we recognise as a newt; though some will not have completed metamorphosis until the following spring.

Newts spend a lot of time on land, but

101

Common Frog

Common Toad

Common Smooth Newt

if you feed them regularly in the same place (say with chopped worms) they can become quite tame.

Bear in mind that newts will eat fish fry, so do not encourage them if you want to raise the maximum number of fish. Adults are not at risk.

Amphibians such as these are interesting visitors to the pond and are generally to be welcomed as they eat slugs, woodlice, and many other garden pests.

TERRAPINS

The chances are that you have never considered keeping terrapins in the pond. Some people are tempted to try, however. If you feel so inclined, it is vital to choose the right type of terrapin, and to provide suitable conditions.

The young red-eared terrapins *(Chrysemys scripta)* often sold in pet or aquarium shops are unsuitable as they need heated conditions. You could, however, try larger specimens, say with a shell over 12.5 cm (5 in) long; but you must bring them in once autumn arrives, and not put them out again until warm weather returns. They are best kept in a small pool on their own (they may attack fish) and you should ideally have a central island where they can emerge to bask in the sun, and you will need a small perimeter fence around the pond to prevent them wandering off.

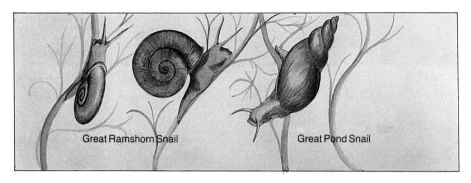

Great Ramshorn Snail   Great Pond Snail

Water snails should be introduced into the pond with caution. The great pond snail will just as happily eat the plants as the algae, and can make unsightly holes in the leaves of plants such as waterlilies. The ramshorn snail is a more harmless species and a better one to introduce if you want snails.

There are two European species, *Clemmys leprosa* and *Emys orbicularis,* which could be tried if terrapins appeal to you.

SNAILS

Snails are controversial. There is a popular belief that the snails will eat up all the rubbish and algae. Other people will not have any snails in the belief that they will eat the plants. As is often the case with conflicting beliefs, there is a grain of truth in both arguments. On the whole one is better off without them, although the great ramshorn snail *(Planorbis corneus)* is likely to confine itself to algae more than plants.

Do not expect any type of snail to have any sort of real impact on algae. They may eat up rotting food left by fish, but they produce their own wastes so it is doubtful that the water is any purer for them. Certainly they are likely to turn their attention to your plants at some point. The one to take pains to remove in British gardens is the great pond snail *(Limnaea stagnalis),* a snail with a large, conical pointed shell and a strong appetite for plants.

MUSSELS

Mussels are hardly worth introducing into the pond; they spend most of their time buried in mud anyway, and at one stage in their life cycle are parasitic on fish. The only time you will need to think about them is if you want to breed Bitterling *(Rhodeus amarus),* a fish that lays its eggs directly into the swan mussel through an ovipositor.

INSECTS

You will find a wide variety of insect life

103

in and around the pond. This book cannot pretend to be a guide to even a fraction of what you may encounter, but there are a few common insects that it is worth knowing; either because they do some good or because they are potentially harmful. They are illustrated on the following two pages.

Giant diving beetle, *Dytiscus marginalis* Both beetle and larvae are ferocious. The prey is seized in the jaws and injected with digestive juices.

Frog tadpoles are a familiar part of the spring scene.

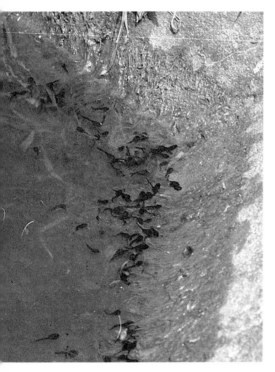

Water boatman There are two kinds. The lesser water boatman *(Corixa punctata)* has middle legs that resemble oars, and the greater water boatman *(Notonecta glauca)* thrusts with powerful elongated hind limbs. They usually swim upside down with characteristic jerky movements. They are predatory and will eat anything, including small fish, up to the size of a tadpole. They may also wound larger fish.

Water scorpion *(Nepa cinerea)* does not have a sting, but it has strong front limbs with which to grasp prey before getting to work with its powerful jaws and sucking the victim dry. You may find them at the edge of the pond, but they are generally difficult to see in the mud.

Dragonflies are an exciting and usually welcome sight. Unfortunately their larvae are ugly, sluggish predators that will grab convenient prey with their strong mouthparts.

Leeches Fish leeches can be a nuisance to fish. If they are numerous, suspend some raw meat into the water on a string. After a while it should have attracted a large number of leeches which can then be destroyed. To remove leech from a fish, hold the fish in a wet cloth and dab salt on the tail of the leech; it should let go!

Hydra These minute, octopus-like jelly creatures live on submerged plants. They catch their prey by paralysing them with

Dragonflies are attractive visitors to the pond, but their nymphs may eat small fish fry.

Much of the natural history of the pond is at microscopic level, and there is no shortage of microscopic life for children to discover.

their stinging tentacles. Mostly they eat things like water fleas (daphnia), but if present in large numbers may affect the population of fry. They are difficult to see and once you lift up the plant they seem to disappear as they form an indistinct gelatinous mass (though they will reappear once returned to the water).

MICROSCOPIC ORGANISMS

You will need specialist books to attempt to identify the teeming microscopic inhabitants of the pond, and even then it

105

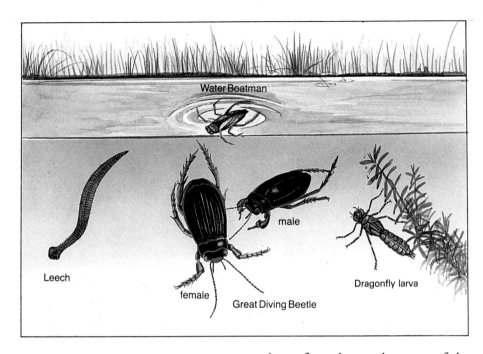

Some of the less attractive inhabitants of the pond *(drawings not to scale)*.

is not easy. It can be fascinating, however, and very educational for children, just looking at the various life forms.

Apart from a microscope you will need slides, cover slips, and a pipette. Draw up a sample of pond water in the pipette, and transfer a *drop* to the centre of the slide. Lower the cover slip carefully, laying one edge on the slide first and then lowering it down carefully. If you just drop it on, trapped air bubbles may affect viewing. Start at the lowest magnification to look at a relatively broad area of the sample, then larger magnification to inspect individual objects of interest.

If you happen to read this chapter first, you may think that water gardening is bad news; but it is important to keep things in perspective. Some of the things discussed in this chapter you may never encounter, and certainly it is most unlikely that more than one or two problems will arise in a year. Mostly they are minor, though green water can be infuriating.

DIRTY WATER

Few problems cause as much anguish as murky water. Not unnaturally most of us expect the water to be sparkling and inviting . . . and of course we expect to be able to see the fish. Because new ponds are particularly liable to turn an uninviting shade of pea soup green, it is understandable that disillusionment can easily set in if this is your first venture into water gardening.

Do not look for the answer in chemical cures; useful though they are in particular circumstances, long-term clear water depends on good pool design and management, not on additives.

Green water is caused by millions of tiny free-floating algae suspended in the water. To get rid of them you must find a way of controlling their growth; chemicals are one way, competition another. The latter is cheaper and longer-lasting.

The best way of 'starving' the algae is to have plenty of other plants competing for both light and nutrients. As a guideline, if you have about a third of the surface covered by floating foliage, the water that you can see should be clear. You must also have sufficient submerged oxygenating plants (see page 79).

Green water is a common problem in new ponds because there is often an abundant supply of minerals in the water from the freshly introduced loam, and the new plants will not yet have grown enough to make use of them, and they will not be providing adequate shade to starve the algae of light. As the desirable plants grow and flourish, conditions should become less favourable for the algae. In the meantime it is well worth considering a chemical control; so that you can enjoy the pond while you are waiting for a natural balance to be achieved, and to give the plants a chance to become established without competition from the algae.

There are also design considerations that will improve matters by providing areas of shade and associated convection currents.

The smaller the pool the more difficulty you are likely to have with green water. A pond with a surface area of less than 2×2 m (say 6×7 ft) is probably going to be much more difficult to 'balance' than a larger one.

There is another filamentous type of algae that can be a nuisance. It grows into a mass that resembles green cotton-wool, and is known as *blanket weed*. It is unsightly rather than a hazard to the plants even though it tends to grow over oxygenators as well as on the sides of the pool.

Blanket weed is likely to be noticed most in spring, before other plants have started to grow and compete. Given time most of it will probably disappear, but you can easily remove unsightly growth by twisting it round a stick to remove it; you can then apply a chemical treatment if you feel that this is necessary. If you are going to use chemical control, it is well worth removing the worst of the blanket weed by hand first; a large quantity of rotting dead algae could starve the water of oxygen.

Chemical control definitely has its uses, but should be regarded as a step towards clean water, not an answer in itself.

You can buy chemicals to control algae in ponds, but do be sure that you buy one suitable for use with fish and plants. It is important to calculate the capacity of your pond first (see page 24) so that you can apply the right amount. If used as directed (you normally dilute the solution first, then apply it to the surface with a sprayer or watering-can, trying to keep it off the plants), your fish and ornamental plants should not be harmed. Some treatments also contain chemicals that will control fungus and white spot diseases on your fish at the same time.

You may find a 'pond block' easier to use. The chemicals are released from the block over a period of weeks (the higher the pH of the water the more slowly it dissolves).

Brown water Dirty-looking brown water is likely to be caused by suspended particles of soil or organic matter. Fish searching in the mud for food are often the cause. Bottom-feeding fish such as tench, as well as carp, are often troublesome in this way; top-feeders such as golden orfe are unlikely to be guilty. To suggest dispensing with the fish would be a harsh solution. But you can do much to improve things by covering exposed areas of loam with a thick layer of gravel. Again there are chemicals that you could try. These cause the particles to sink to the bottom again, but of course they will not remove the basic cause.

Filters You can keep your pond clear and healthy with filters, perhaps connected to the cascade or fountain plumbing. These are by no means essential if you get the size and natural balance of your pond right, but they are well worth considering if you are keeping fish such as Koi carp, especially if the population is high for the area of water. You may also

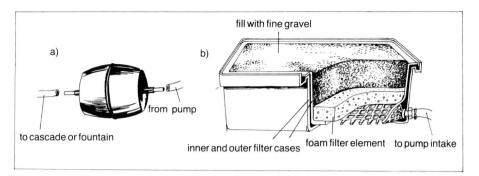

a)

to cascade or fountain

from pump

b)

fill with fine gravel

inner and outer filter cases   foam filter element   to pump intake

These are two simple and relatively inexpensive filters. It is possible to buy more elaborate filters, which are placed outside the pool.

find a pool filter invaluable if you have a small pool (say under 40 sq ft) that is difficult to balance and tends to remain cloudy.

An under-gravel filter is built into the pond itself, which means that it has to be deeper to allow for this, and acts like an under-gravel aquarium filter. It will need a continuously running air pump to provide a supply of oxygen for the bacteria that will break down the waste material. Making a filter of this type is rather a chore and a commitment, and the use of chemicals to treat the fish may affect the efficiency of the bacteria, so for most people one of the alternatives is more practical.

An external filter draws the water by a pump and returns it to the pond treated. You can make an external filter by constructing a series of chambers with increasingly smaller gravel in each one, finishing with silver sand. The inlet should be at a relatively high level, the

outlet pipe low down (and of wider bore to avoid the risk of flooding).

Unless you enjoy experimenting and making things yourself, it is better to buy a ready-made filter. A submerged filter for a small pool will have a pipe that you connect to a submersible pump, perhaps used to feed a cascade or a fountain. A typical one will have a foam filter element that you cover with fine gravel. It will only fit certain pumps without some kind of adaptor. There are other types of filter, some that you install at the outlet end of the pump (perhaps at the head of a cascade). These all vary in efficiency. You must be clear about whether they are simply straining out large debris, to keep pumps clear for instance, or biological filters in which harmful waste products are also broken down by bacteria.

A good biological filter will operate outside the pool, perhaps hidden near the top of a waterfall, and the processed water allowed to discharge into the cascade. Alternatively, it can be placed close to the pool and the water simply cycled through from a pump. A typical biological filter has a tank with a lid, and thick layers of open-celled foam, inlet, outlet and overflow pipes, and possibly a control valve.

Biological filters must operate continuously (at least during the summer; they are not needed in winter) because if the filter medium is allowed to dry out or become starved of oxygen and water, the beneficial purifying bacteria will die.

Filters of this type will hold back solids immediately, but the biological action will take about a month to become effective. The filter foam will need cleaning occasionally. You will need piping of the right diameter, so check these details when ordering.

AILING FISH

Provided that you quarantine fish before you put them into the pond, and make sure that only healthy stock is introduced, fish pests and diseases are unlikely to be a big problem. Inevitably there will be some casualties.

If a fish does need treatment for a specific trouble, it is best to remove it to a small 'hospital' pool or a fish tank. This will make treatment easier and reduce the risk of an infectious disease or parasites spreading to other fish in the meantime.

One of the most infuriating causes of fish loss is so-called oxygen starvation, for which a change of environment is the answer rather than any chemical treatment. If fish are gasping at the surface, especially in hot, thundery weather,

this is a sign that the pond is overcrowded, or that fish that need a high level of oxygen (such as dace and golden orfe) are suffering because the water is not aerated enough. Actually the cause of death is not so much lack of oxygen as a lethal dose of carbon dioxide, which in thundery weather is not exchanged for oxygen at the normal rate. For the latter, a waterfall or a fountain might be enough to overcome the problem. As an emergency, churn up the surface with a jet of water from a hose. Simply adding more oxygenating plants is not the answer because plants release carbon dioxide at night and make matters worse; which is why the fish are often found dead in the morning. This kind of loss is tragic because they are healthy one day, dead the next.

Body rot Ulceration of the body. A bad form of this is known as 'hole in the body', which indicates the magnitude of the problem. *Treatment:* antibiotics are the best hope, but the disease is often fatal. It might be worth giving the pond a slow water change.

Fin rot Ragged fins with frayed edges, while the fish appears dull, may be caused by a bacterial infection. Long-finned goldfish are susceptible to this if left outside in very cold weather. *Treatment:* antibiotics are likely to be the most successful.

Fungal infections show up as cotton-wool-like patches in the fins or body; in water containing a lot of green algae the growth may be stained green and look rather like blanket weed. They often follow some kind of injury. *Treatment:* add 6 g of cooking salt to 1 litre of water (1 oz to 1 gallon), and immerse the fish in this for half an hour each day. Use a thermometer to ensure that the treatment bath is the same temperature as the pond or tank. If the fish seems unduly distressed, remove it immediately.

Mouth fungus Actually caused by a bacterium, not a fungus. Off-white growths around the mouth area gradually erode the tissue of the mouth. The fish refuses to eat. *Treatment:* antibiotics are the best treatment, though proprietary treatments which are more easily available can be used. It is also worth giving the pond a slow water change before treating.

White spot A common problem caused by a protozoan. The parasite burrows into the skin and causes white spots about the size of a pinhead all over the fish. It can weaken the fish and prove fatal if untreated. *Treatment:* fortunately the problem can be treated successfully provided you are aware that the disease is there. Use a proprietary remedy and repeat three or four days later to make sure the parasites have been eliminated. If you have just a few fish it is best to treat them in a tank or other container, and leave the pool free of fish for a week; by which time the parasite will have been unable to survive without fish.

Anchor worm These look like a piece of thread about 6 mm (¼ in) long attached to the side of the fish. They may cause lesions and tumour-like growths. Actually they are crustaceans not worms. *Treatment:* hold the fish in a wet cloth and apply a concentrated solution of potassium permanganate (or you can use paraffin) with a small paintbrush. The parasites can then be pulled away with tweezers and the wound dabbed with an antiseptic disinfectant such as iodine solution. Once in the pond, it may take two months for all stages of them to die out, assuming no fish are left in the pool.

Flukes These are small and difficult to spot. They often affect the gills. A fish that rubs itself against rocks or other objects should be suspect. If they affect the gills, which may be pallid, the fish may gasp. *Treatment:* there are proprietary remedies that are effective. You may have to repeat the treatment, perhaps five times at intervals of a few days to be sure of eliminating the various stages. Orfe may react adversely to some treatments for flukes.

Fish lice There are several kinds, but they usually have almost transparent or light green or brown bodies about 6 mm (¼ in) across, and look rather like tiny plaice. They attach themselves to their hosts with feelers. The fish are likely to jump and twitch. *Treatment:* treat as described for anchor worms.

Red pest The belly looks red as the

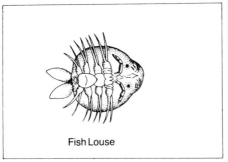

Fish Louse

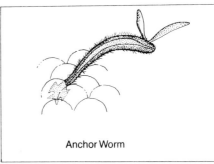

Anchor Worm

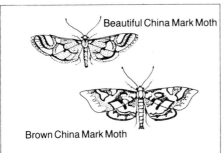

Beautiful China Mark Moth

Brown China Mark Moth

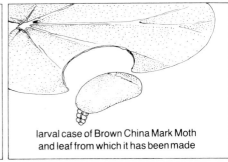

larval case of Brown China Mark Moth
and leaf from which it has been made

blood vessels become engorged. The gills may be affected. The fish may become sluggish. It is an infectious bacterial disease. *Treatment:* often a sign of over-crowding. Improve the environment, and ensure adequate circulation of water. If possible leave the pool fishless for a couple of months before restocking.

Swimbladder disorders　A fish that appears to have difficulty swimming to the surface is probably suffering from a swimbladder disorder. This can be the result of low temperatures, or of a digestive problem. *Treatment:* transfer the fish to a tank with just enough water to cover it adequately, and do not feed it for a week.

A form of disorder known as carp swimbladder disease affects young fish, the air bladder becoming filled with debris, affecting its function. The cause is uncertain so there is no effective treatment.

Tuberculosis　Piscine tuberculosis is a chronic disease that causes the fish to lose weight and become thin. It is contagious and affected fish must be isolated immediately.

HERONS

Herons may seem an irrelevance to a city-dweller, but if you live in a rural area where your pond may be on their flight-path, they are anything but a joke. If they do not clear your pond of fish at the first attempt they are likely to return regularly, probably at dawn before you notice them.

Do not assume that if you live in a town you are exempt from this worry; if there is countryside nearby, you may still be paid a visit by this beautiful but unwelcome bird.

You may wonder why heron ornaments are sometimes used in ponds; one would think they might attract the real thing. Apparently they are respecters of each other's territory and it is said that if the real heron see what it thinks is a heron already feeding it will fly on.

Mostly the precautions are more pragmatic. Herons do not land directly in the water, but at the edge; then they wade in. So providing some kind of barrier at the edge may be enough to solve the problem, and is far better than covering the pond with a net, which detracts enormously from the visual appeal of the pond, and completely spoils the plants.

Some fish enthusiasts who suffer from the attentions of herons (and just the occasional visit is all that is necessary to lose most of your stock) use an electrified wire around the edge, supported on old car sparking plugs. It is switched on each night and keeps both herons and cats at a safe distance from the fish. A simpler alternative for most of us is a row of small canes about 15 cm (6 in) high, with black cotton or fishing line strung between them to make a low barrier. This will usually upset the heron enough as he tries to wade in to persuade him to try elsewhere.

PLANT PROBLEMS

Fortunately plant pests and diseases are probably less of a problem in a pond than in the rest of the garden. The drawback is that most garden chemicals must not be used near the pool. Description of the pests mentioned below are not included as they are illustrated on p. 106 and 112, and seeing a pest is always a better aid to identification than a description.

China mark moth There are two species that may be troublesome, the brown China mark moth *(Nymphula stagnata)* and the beautiful China mark moth *(N. nympheata)*. The former cuts and shreds the leaves of aquatic plants to provide itself with a shelter in which it weaves a silky cocoon. The eggs are laid in late summer in rows along the edge of the leaves of aquatic plants. The caterpillars emerge and burrow beneath the foliage and later cut out pieces of foliage to stick on the underside of the leaves. They hibernate for the winter and reappear in spring when they weave their cocoons before pupating.

The beautiful China mark moth has caterpillars that burrow into the stems of aquatic plants, where they hibernate. *Control:* hand-picking is the only practical control. Net pieces of floating leaves that could have cocoons attached.

Blanket weed can be unsightly. Chemical control is possible, but the largest bits are best removed with a stick or rake first.

Caddis flies There are many types of caddis fly, and the larvae of all of them are likely to feed on the foliage of aquatic plants. The eggs become attached to plants in the water and after about ten days the larvae hatch and construct themselves shelters from debris. They feed on the leaves, stems, roots or flowers. They pupate in the pool or among plants at the water's edge, to emerge as moth-like in-

Some believe that a heron will not land if it sees another heron already there. If this works using a model is an attractive way to protect the pool.

114

sects with grey or brown wings. There is not a lot that you can do about them, but fish should achieve reasonable control.

Waterlily aphid A fairly common pest, affecting all succulent aquatic plants as well as waterlilies. These aphids, like blackfly in this case, need little description, and like all aphids they breed prodigiously. The waterlily aphid overwinters on cherry or plum trees. *Control:* try to attack the overwintering stage if you have cherry or plum trees by spraying them with a tar oil winter wash. The only sensible control in the summer if you have desirable fish in the pond is to hose them off with a jet of water and hope that the fish eat them. You may be able to weight the topgrowth beneath the water for a day, though much depends on how 'flexible' the plant is for this treatment.

Waterlily beetle A difficult pest, but fortunately not a widespread problem. The shiny black larvae of the beetle strip the epidermis from the lily leaves, which then start to rot. *Control:* spray affected pads forcibly with a jet of water, or submerge the foliage for 24 hours, then with luck they will be eaten by the fish. If no fish are present, use an insecticide such as malathion.

Waterlily leaf spot The rot causes dark brown patches on the lily leaves, which eventually rot and disintegrate. It is worse in damp, humid weather. *Control:* remove and burn affected leaves.

Waterlily root rot Waterlilies with dark or mottled foliage appear to be particularly susceptible. Leaf and flower stems become soft and blackened, and the roots rot and smell foul. *Control:* remove affected plants as soon as they are noticed, and destroy them. If valuable waterlilies are threatened, remove all fish and treat the water with copper sulphate. Tie the crystals in a muslin bag attached to a cane, and swish this through water until the crystals have completely dissolved. However, getting the dose right is not easy and it is better to give waterlilies a miss for a year, then start again.

ICY WEATHER

One thing fairly sure to send the new pond owner into a paroxysm of anxiety is a long hard frost that forms a thick layer of ice over the pool. Usually there is little to worry about, but ice is not without risks so it has to be considered as a potential problem.

A thin sheet of ice that lasts for two or three days should cause no harm. A thick sheet of ice that lasts for more than say three days needs to be taken more seriously. A shallow pool or a small raised pond made from say a half-barrel or a plastic container could possibly freeze solid in very severe weather, and although some fish seem to come through this experience unscathed, it may be too much for young fish.

Much more of a problem, however, is the risk of a build-up of toxic gases beneath the ice, especially if there is a lot of rotting vegetation in the pond. The surface of the water is the pond's lung through which oxygen is absorbed and waste gases released. If that does not work properly the fish may suffer, regardless of the depth of the water.

It will be impossible to keep a large area of pond ice-free (breaking the ice could distress the fish, and letting lumps of ice float about may only chill the water more). The best you can hope to do is keep a small area of water open; just enough for the pond to 'breath'. How to

You can buy both mains and low-voltage pond heaters. These are by far the most satisfactory way of keeping a small area of water open during a prolonged spell of freezing weather.

do it is another matter. Most people will tell you to float a large ball on the water before it freezes. The theory is that the ball absorbs some of the pressure from the ice (more important in a concrete pond), and removing the ball will expose a small patch of open water. In reality, in severe weather the ball will simply rise up as ice forms beneath it. When you remove the ball, there will be a slight rounded depression in the ice, but the pond will still be frozen over. In thin ice, tapping the ball will break the ice, but not if the ice is thick.

A hole can be made gently by standing a kettle or pan of hot water on the ice (be prepared to change the water several times); but within an hour ice will

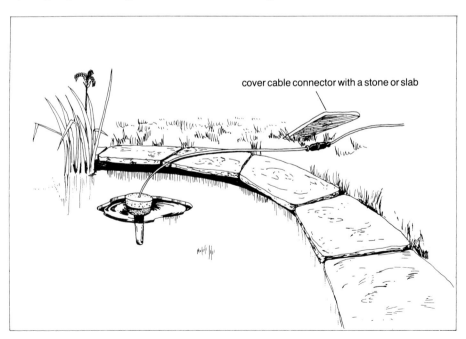

cover cable connector with a stone or slab

An electrified wire to protect a pond from cats and herons. Old car sparking plugs have been adapted to carry the wire.

Large-mesh netting is another way to deter herons, but you may not like the visual impact of the netting.

If you do not have a pond heater, try using a pan of hot water to produce a hole in the ice if it has been frozen over for several days. Tie a string to it in case it sinks when the ice melts through.

probably have re-formed over the area.

The hole made will enable you to scoop or siphon out an inch or so of water beneath the ice – which theoretically is less likely to freeze because the layer of air between ice and water provides a form of insulation. Again, life is not always as predicted, and if you keep on doing this, there will be less and less unfrozen water for the fish.

There is really only one dependable solution: a pond heater. You can buy low-voltage pond heaters if you are worried about using a direct mains supply. A pond heater will keep only a small area of water open, but that is all you need, and it will not be very expensive to run.

119

10·CLEANING, RENOVATING AND REPAIRING

Ponds do not need a lot of maintenance, and there is no need to regard cleaning the pond as a ritual that has to be carried out once a year. It is unlikely to be necessary more frequently than every second year, and probably less frequently than this. There comes a time, however, when the plants become overgrown and the water contaminated with accumulated debris and leaves.

You are unlikely to let your own pond fall into a neglected state, but sometimes when you move home you inherit a pond that is in need of renovation rather than a mere clean out. Of course leaks do happen and then repairs are necessary.

CLEANING OUT THE POND

Some old concrete ponds have a plug at the bottom by which you can theoretically drain the pond. Even if it has one, the job of groping round for it is off-putting (very few have a special chamber and key for the job), and even then the outlet may be clogged. More importantly, if you use the drain it may destabilise the ground beneath the pond which could lead to the risk of cracking later.

The real choice is to siphon or to pump. If you can take a hose to a lower point, possibly to a drain, siphoning is a simple approach, but you risk losing some small fish along with the water unless you use some kind of filter. Usually you will have to use a pump. The one for your fountain or cascade will do; just connect a hose from the pump to some suitable spot in the garden or to a drain. A pump is not going to get that last drop of water out, of course, because as soon as the water level drops to the pump inlet you will have to abandon this method and finish off with a bucket.

It makes sense to net as many fish as possible before you start emptying, but as the mud will get stirred up you will inevitably have to rescue the last of them as the water level drops. The best place for the fish while you clean out and replant the pond is in a cool, shady place, perhaps in a garage. Relatively shallow containers with a large surface area are best, but cover them with netting to prevent fish jumping out or cats jumping in.

Keep any snails that you want to return separately in a large bucket. Keep those with flat, catherine-wheel type shells carried upright on their back (these feed on algae). Discard snails with pointed shells, as they may eat waterlilies and other aquatics.

A pond should not need cleaning out more frequently than every couple of years. Most of the water can be pumped out, but the last few inches will probably have to be scooped out with a bucket.

If a liner is used, be careful not to damage it by treading on stones, and scrub the liner clean with a brush.

Remove the plants and scrub the inside of the pool. Rinse and empty the water, then refill with clean water. Replant the lilies after washing them and cutting away old roots and tubers, keeping only the strongest shoots attached to healthy tubers. Wash the aquatic plants with a very mild solution of permanganate of potash (add just enough crystals to turn the liquid a pale pink). Replant them in fresh soil. Ordinary heavy garden soil will do, but make sure it has not been fertilised recently; nor should it contain manure or garden compost.

You will need to allow the fresh water to stand for a few days before returning the fish.

LEAKY AND NEGLECTED PONDS

A leaky or overgrown pool is disheartening and an eyesore. The choice is to fill it in or renovate it. As you are presumably interested in water gardening the latter course will have the most appeal.

The time to renovate an old pond is in the summer, when you can see what plants are there and are better able to assess the problems. Leaks are also easier to detect in the summer because in winter the water table may be high and high rainfall may mask small leaks.

It will be easier to find the leak with the water in (unless the fault lies at the bottom). Fill it up with water, and mark

A butyl rubber liner is easy to repair or join with a kit that you can buy. The liner to be joined or repaired must be cleaned thoroughly first.

The patching material has a protective film that has to be peeled away before you use it.

A special adhesive is brushed on. Wear protective gloves.

The patch is simply pressed into place over the prepared surface.

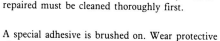

(Left) If you inherit an overgrown pond like this one it is best to think about clearing it out and renovating it, even though it may be a big job.

the point at which the water stabilises (you may need to give it a few days if the leak is slow). The bottom of the crack or slit should be at about that level, so inspect the pond carefully to isolate the problem. If you mark the water level you can do this once the pond is empty if this is more convenient.

The pond will have to be emptied, and the fish rehoused as described for cleaning a pond.

Be ruthless about the fish. Check them all for signs of disease, and treat any that are likely to respond to treatment; humanely destroy any that are not likely to be cured. Take no risk about re-introducing pests and diseases back into the pond. Dispose of catfish and stickle-backs (they may have become introduced into your pond by accident even if you did not actually buy them). Uncoloured goldfish and carp (usually dark brown) should be removed, otherwise with further breeding future generations may deteriorate further. Bear in mind that young fish less than a couple of years old may not yet have assumed their final colouring, so do not discard those less than about 5 cm (2 in long).

Plants need even more ruthless sorting out. If the pond has been neglected for some time, three or four strong species may have overtaken the choicer kinds. Plants likely to do this are the reedmaces *Typha angustifolia* and *T. latifolia;* burr reed, *Sparganium ramosum;* Canadian pond weed, *Elodea canadensis;* and water mint, *Mentha aquatica.* Bear this in mind if ever planting these species in a pond.

They are probably best discarded completely unless you are prepared to keep them in careful and regular check.

Duckweeds should be eliminated if at all possible (easier said than done as small pieces tend to get in among the plants that you want to save). If oxygenating plants such as elodea have choked the pond, it is best to remove the lot and take some 15 cm (6 in) long cuttings, which should root if you insert them in a small pot of garden soil (submerged of course).

Waterlilies are almost always worth saving unless they are the rampant native *Nymphaea alba.*

Do not be tempted to re-use any of the soil removed from the pond. Replant everything, washing the plants (leaves and roots) with a hose and replanting in fresh compost. If you do not do this you will probably put pests and diseases back in the pond. The mud and soil from the pond will soon dry out and can be spread over the garden or put on the compost heap.

Repairing a liner   If a butyl liner has a slit or hole, it should be possible to make a good repair. You can buy a special adhesive and a length of patch (usually sold by the metre or yard), and the repair is made rather as you would mend a cycle inner tube puncture. The liner must of course be absolutely clean and dry before you put on the patch.

PVC liners are worth repairing if only a few years old (again you can buy a repair kit), but if it is already say 10 years old, when it is likely to start deteriorating

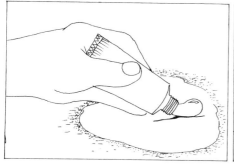

You can buy a special kind of sealer/adhesive for repairing vinyl sheets. These are widely available as they are used for children's paddling pools and other jobs besides pond repairs. The area is cleaned and the tear covered with the substance first, then a patch fixed in place if necessary. The job is quick and easy, the repair effective.

anyway, you might consider putting in a new liner.

If you have saved some of the trimmings from the liner when the pond was installed, you do not need to buy a kit. Apply a PVC adhesive (these are widely available) to the cleaned area, leave it for a minute or two to become tacky, then press the patch firmly into place. Try to keep some pressure on it. You should be able to refill the pond after about an hour.

Patches are not likely to be successful on brittle areas above the water line, and there is no use trying to patch a porous old liner.

Polythene liners cannot be repaired.

Repairing a rigid plastic or GRP pool Rigid plastic pools cannot really

be repaired satisfactorily. Glass-fibre (glass-reinforced plastic – GRP) pools can be repaired if they have a crack. You will probably have to lift the pool to make a good job of it. Use a repair kit sold for car body work (it will contain a resin that you mix with a catalyst, which you brush on to layers of glass-fibre matt over the damaged area). Follow the instructions on the kit; the surface must be clean, and the work done in a warm, dry atmosphere.

Cracks in glass-fibre are rare, but they can result from projecting stones in the ground or very heavy rockery stones on the rim. Avoid these risks when replacing the pool.

Repairing a concrete pool Concrete pools should last for very many years if properly constructed, but poor construction can lead to problems very quickly. If the pool has flaked badly, there is not much that you can do. The best solution is to clean it out and cover it with a liner. You may need to place layers of newspaper or perhaps old carpet or vinyl flooring over the surface to

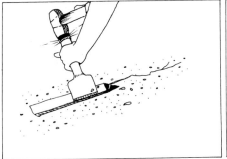 

Small cracks in concrete need to be enlarged before refilling.

prevent rough concrete damaging the liner.

Large fractures are also best regarded as marking the end of a concrete pond's life; even if you make a repair the spot is likely to remain a source of weakness. It is perhaps best to fill the fracture and to use a liner.

Straightforward cracks can be dealt with. Using a cold chisel and club hammer, chip out more of the concrete to make a V-shaped channel, making sure the surface is rough so that the new concrete can key onto it. A mix of one part cement, two parts sand and four parts gravel (by volume) is the normal mix, but if you are in a hurry to complete the repair a quick-drying cement can be used. You will also need to add a waterproof bonding agent (ask your builder's merchant for advice).

Brush the crack with water before you apply the concrete. It will take several days to set properly, then it can be painted over with a neutralising agent to deal with the free lime that might otherwise harm the fish.

To be on the safe side, paint the repaired area with a pond sealant, making sure you overlap the old concrete. You can get suitable sealants from a water garden specialist.

It will be about a fortnight before it is safe to return fish to a repaired concrete pond (unless of course you have used a liner).

INDEX

127